2546½

THE god OF ROCK

WARNING!

PLEASE READ THIS ENTIRE BOOK. Otherwise, the message will be misunderstood and the messenger misinterpreted.

This book is a primer designed to educate Christian parents and teens to the spiritual, mental, and physical danger of being distracted from the Lordship of Christ by the addicting power of rock music.

The formula for examining ones listening habits is in the expanded section.

DEDICATION

To Brent and Holly Haynes, my teenagers, for their love and constant support of my ministry. Brent, you are a wonderful son and a good friend. Holly, you are the daughter of a father's dreams. Thank you for being you and being mine at the same time.

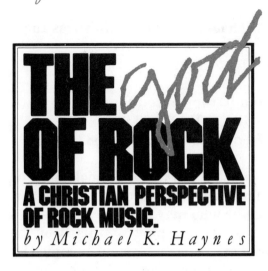

THE *god* OF ROCK
A CHRISTIAN PERSPECTIVE OF ROCK MUSIC.
by Michael K. Haynes

PUBLISHED BY

MINISTRIES AND PUBLICATIONS
P.O. Box 1254
Lindale, Texas 75771

All scripture verses used are from the King James version of the Bible.

COVER DESIGN: BRANDAL DESIGN

APPEARING ON COVER: TERRY TAYLOR

1st Printing 1982
2nd Printing 1983
3rd Printing 1984

CONTENTS

Ephesians 5:11—14 "... And have no fellowship with the unfruitful works of darkness, but rather reprove (expose) them. For it is a shame even to speak of those things which are done of them in secret. But all things that are reproved are made mainfest by the light: for whatsoever doth make manifest is light. Wherefore he saith, Awake thou that sleepest, and arise from the dead, and Christ shall give thee light."

A special thank you to Scott Burgess and Greg Dillard for their help in research and running down albums —also for their disc jockey expertise.

A very special thank you to my son, Brent Haynes, for his presence during the final stages of my research.

A special thank you to Dr. Richard Kirgan, my pastor, for the title to the book.

Another thank you to my wife for her concept involving the cover.

Thanks to Donnette Goheen and Rebekah Lagrone, very good secretaries.

A special thank you to Larry and Tracy White for their unselfish involvement in this ministry.

A PERSONAL TESTIMONY

I would like to be able to say that I am writing from the standpoint of an authority on the subject of music. This is, however, not exactly the case. The fact of the matter is that I played music professionally for a period of ten years before coming to my senses. During this time I met and played with people who have since become very successful in the music industry. It is with reluctance, but out of necessity, that I share some of my experiences with you.

I began to play for pay in Ft. Polk, Louisiana. While in the Army, some members of my unit and I decided the salary we were getting from Uncle Sam just wasn't enough. So, we formed a band and began to play in local clubs. We played in the Leesville, Louisiana, area and all parts surrounding. This section of our country is very much in the hands of the evil one. South Louisiana is noted for its fighting music and "bawdy" houses.

When I received my discharge, I made up my mind that I wanted to continue as a professional musician. I was married at the time of this decision, and simply did not know that the lifestyle of a "player" was not conducive to a good marriage...to say the least.

I was at the ripe old age of twenty-one when I began to look for my "pie in the sky." The year was 1961. Music was becoming the artform of the future...the vehicle through which to speak. Being an angry young man myself, I felt that I had as much right to regurgitate my stored-up venom as anyone. However, I quickly found that in order to make any money, I had to play what others wanted to hear, not what would necessarily allow me to express myself.

At the time, nightclubs were better outlets for musicians like me. While others were making it through the airway routes, I was bound to the club scene. I was locked up night after night with hundreds of empty faces. Although several times I tried to break into a broader market with my music, it never happened. After a while, I made peace with my plight, and began to live in the dirt with the people who paid to escape through dancing, drinking, doping and all that goes with that scene.

I had become the main force behind several musicians. I was the band "manager," so to speak. I got the gigs ... signed the contracts ... kept the books ... made the deals, etc. Our group was fast becoming one of the more popular club bands in Texas. We had great talent. The group's members were second to none as gifted musicians. Actually, if it had not been for my business expertise, I might have lost my job. The band was good ... very good! We backed numerous "name" singers in sessions and on the road. We were making music for a living.

As time went on, I found myself becoming inextricably involved in an underworld life. Playing all night in clubs was so commonplace that I could not see what I was doing to everyone around me — especially my wife. The club scene was not "her thing." She hated every minute of this horrible lifestyle I had developed. She didn't know whether I would come home stoned, angry, depressed, or any combination thereof.

One night in particular, she locked me out of the house. When I arrived home, I methodically smashed every window (including doors), climbed in one of them, and went to bed. Many was the night that I came in after having been in a fight. To this day, I do not know what held our marriage together.

We were on our way to becoming casualties when something happened in our lives. After two years of my being on the road, our son was born. I was playing in a club in Lawton, Oklahoma, immediately before his birth. I thought to myself, "What a clod you are, Haynes." I realized, probably for the first time, that I was going to be a father ... and a pretty sorry one at that. I felt so bad about the mess I had made of my life that I decided to stop playing. I broke a union contract with the club, gave my regards to the band, and headed home to be with my wife.

Please be aware, however, that playing music gets into your blood. When one has played as long as I had, quitting is no easy matter. I know why now ... but the since-acquired insight didn't help me then. I turned over all the new leaves that a repentant musician might turn over, but to no avail. I still had to play music. The original group never really got it back together after I left, but that didn't stop me from doing one-night stands as a "Drummer for Hire." I was doing anything to "make it" in music. I saw it as my chance to be *somebody*.

My wife was ashamed of my musical involvement, and rightly so. She hardly mentioned it around her friends. She would say, "Please, Michael, get some kind of a job that I can relate to." And ...she said much more than that. Consequently, I got the message. I took a "daytime" job at J.C. Penney Company selling clothes. I remember making $37.50 a week at the store, and $200 to $300 a night playing music. Of course, my playing was cut down to one night a week, but that had to suffice ...at least I didn't have to give it up altogether.

Without relating all of the details of my entire testimony, let me simply say that our loving Lord saw fit to deliver me from what could have been a total disaster for Michael K. Haynes. He, over a period of time, set me free from the degradation of the life that a club musician must lead in order to make a living.

Several of the people with whom I played still do the same thing. Their lives have seen no change in years...still the same music, the same dances, the same clubs, and the same emptiness. I see some of them from time to time. It always refreshes me to see what God lifted me from, but saddens me because there is seemingly nothing that I can do for them. Let me put it a bit plainer...there is nothing that they *want* me to do for them. They are lost! Very, very LOST!

It would be impossible for me to describe all of the events of those years. I would be hard-pressed to even remember. You see, the Lord erased a major portion of the horror and utter despair that I felt during my playing days. He left only enough memory for me to be able to truly praise Him for His saving grace. The sole reason for sharing any of my experiences of being a "player" is to let you, the reader, know that I do know something of which I speak. I am certainly not proud of my actions during that period of my life, but I am sure that our Lord can work for good all of those miserable but valuable experiences.

MKH

CHAPTER ONE
PARENTS... YOU JUST DON'T KNOW

The time was 1:00 p.m. The day was Saturday. The scene was The Superbowl of Rock. It was the final stage of my research for this book. When the gates to the Bowl opened, we began immediately to perform the duties we were contracted to conduct. My son, Brent, and I were working as medics for an outdoor Rock concert with an expected attendance of 70,000. The weather forecast said sunny and extremely hot. It called for approximately 115° on the plastic-coated lawn of the Bowl. This would mean hundreds of young people would be overcome by heat. This would also mean that scores of other young people would be hauled out of the concert due to respiratory arrest, drug overdose, drunkenness, fighting, falling, being trampled, and assorted other extremes. It all happened!

I am now completely sure that most parents have no idea what goes on at an outdoor Rock concert. If they did, it would probably cut into the attendance considerably. For example, the night before the concert, kids come from miles around just to camp in parking lots adjacent to the Bowl. They smoke pot, get drunk, place their speakers on top of their cars or vans and turn them to the loudest possible volume, and in many instances...have sex. You see, the concert gives them the excuse to be there! Otherwise, the police would not permit such mass loitering.

Yet, there they were! A sea of vehicles and kids! Speakers were blaring, and all on different tapes or stations. It sounded like noise from hell itself.

We made our initial rounds early. We knew that the gates were not to be opened until 1:00 p.m. This meant that kids would already be primed for doing what is called "normal concert activity." I'll have to be honest! I wasn't ready for what I was about to see! The last concert I had attended was in 1972 as a guest of a member of ZZ Top, a very popular band. My, how things have progressed! Back then things were bad enough, but it is difficult to describe what goes on in the present!

"What *is* a Rock concert?" one may ask. How are they put on? Who does the behind-the-scenes promotion? How much money is involved? In other words, does someone just bring a couple or three bands together and invite the crowd? Absolutely NOT! It is a BIG BUSINESS AND BIG BUCKS!

Brent and I went up one day early to see some of the behind-the-scenes activity. There were hundreds of laborers on various crews setting up such things as stage, sound system (the sound system was two stories tall and 50 to 60 yards wide ... and we were told this was a small one), dressing rooms, catering services, tee-shirt security, the hospital and medical stations, hundreds of yards of special fencing for the purpose of herding the kids, and I could go on and on. My sources of information, who would rather remain anonymous, told me that, depending on the company who is promoting the concert, the initial set up cost could be as high as $400,000.

Of course, the Rock stars themselves get the royal treatment. They can demand almost anything they desire, and the promoters grant their wishes. I can see how this would be an absolute must! For example, hypothetically, a promotion company has spent an initial half million dollars for set-up and promo, and sold 70,000 tickets at $18.00 per person. The crowd becomes restless, and some half-stoned maniac, who thinks he is a god, decides he doesn't want to perform! In the first place, the crowd could tear the arena apart! If that happened, the promotion company would stand to lose its initial investment and would never be allowed to put on a concert in that particular place again. You see, these demented musicians know this. Consequently, it is less expensive and certainly less hassle if the promoters simply cater to their assorted sordid whims.

One hears all sorts of rumors, but some of them are actually true. For instance, one particular group (no names) ordered 12 limos to pick up their luggage. Another group ordered several cases of very expensive champagne to be chilled to 73°. When the champagne arrived, one of the members opened a bottle and took a drink. He spewed the beverage out of his mouth and yelled, "I said 73°, this is 74°!" He then proceeded to smash every bottle against the wall.

Of course, there are the girls who literally give themselves to superstar musicians for the privilege of being backstage. Some Rock groups get young girls in the dressing rooms and put live fish and other foreign objects into their bodies. This type of bizarre behavior actually goes on!

I am aware that some will say that material of this shocking nature should *not* be in print! WHY NOT??? PARENTS —— PASTORS —— WHY NOT? It *is* happening, and most of us have had our heads in the dirt long enough! We *could* put a stop to the ruining of young lives in this manner. Other countries have done it! Rock has been banned in several Eastern cultures. Drugs are not a problem in several Eastern countries. *WE* MUST WAKE UP!! YES... IT *IS* HAPPENING!!! YES... WE *NEED* TO KNOW ABOUT IT!!! This is no joke. We are in a war, Christians. OPEN YOUR EYES.

Pastors, if you don't know what Rock is all about, FIND OUT. Ask your young people what they know about it. It will "blow your mind" to find what is just *commonplace* news with them. Bring in an expert... DO SOMETHING! Young people are jumping on THE DOWNBOUND TRAIN by the millions! Why *not* address the issue!

I thought when the Lord directed me to write this book over two years ago that it would probably be a very unpopular message. However, what I did not know was that THE DEVIL WOULD KICK ME IN THE TEETH AS HE HAS! *Praise God for the power of the Cross.* But make no mistake about it, this is definitely frontline "stuff."

The stadium Rock phenomenon in this country is lasciviousness in mass expression. The gates had not been opened for thirty minutes when already the floor of the Bowl was full of young people. Bikinis were the more conservative dress of the hour. My son and I began to make our rounds. May I relate only a few instances of our experience during the course of the day.

We were backstage when someone cried, "Medics!" We ran over and a young grounds-crew member said, "There is someone in the dressing room of Ozzy Osbourne who has twisted his ankle very badly. Could you come?"

We hastened to the dressing room, and as we were walking in, straight down the hall, about 25 feet in front of us were two young girls, partially nude, standing in front of the mirrors blow-drying their hair. I thought I was in the wrong dressing room for a moment, and I turned to Brent who was behind me, looking sort of startled himself.

Then we heard a cry from around the corner, "Come on ... this guy is in pain." We ignored the girls —— who also ignored us —— and found the victim lying on a table. We learned he was the caterer for the bands. He had been chasing one of the young groupies (rock prostitutes) and slipped on some steps. We put ice on the ankle and applied an ace bandage.

We then began to look around. Much to my amazement, the dressing rooms, which were initially football locker rooms, were made to look like plush penthouses. They had been decorated strictly for the rock musicians, to their specifications, I might add. There were all sorts of delicacies, drinks of many kinds, and young girls lying everywhere. We were not allowed to stay long, but what I saw was enough to give me the general impression that these guys were not "hurting" for carnal delight.

After leaving the dressing rooms, we picked up a young man who was stoned *completely* out of his mind. His eyes were rolled back in his head so far that only the whites showed. He was throwing up all over everything...us included. He wore only cutoffs, and had his crotch full of ice. We put him on the cart used for hospital transportation and began to head toward the aid station.

We were stopped in the process and directed to a young girl in the crowd who had experienced respiratory arrest. She was high on drugs, overcome by heat, and unconscious. We placed her next to the guy who was still throwing up and continued to the aid station.

When we arrived, the young man was taken to the doctor who immediately said, "He's drunk! Get a cop!" The police came in, the young man got violent, some medics subdued him, and he was off to jail. The young girl, however, was in worse shape and had to be taken to the hospital.

Brent and I went back to the main floor. By this time there were more people. Consequently, more nudity, drunkenness and fighting. The sweet smell of pot filled the air.

We began to make another round through the crowd. We had just started when we heard, "Medics!" We looked, and a young girl had fallen several flights of steps while coming into the Bowl. We ran for a stretcher and finally got her loaded. She was very scantily dressed, and as we moved through the crowd carrying her to the aid station, guys would reach to touch and fondle her. There were "wolf cries" and other obscenities being shouted. We had to call for tee-shirt security to get us through.

When I refer to tee-shirt security, I mean 200 to 300 very large young men who had been imported to serve as a sort of concert police force. Uniformed policemen will not come into the arena of an outdoor concert for fear of being pelted with bottles, shoes, or other objects. So, the promoters use very "big dudes" who come in and work, mainly because they like to fight. Some of them look like they are from Muscle Beach, California. I understand that many times motorcycle gangs are used because they get their kicks from hurting people. Tee-shirt security is looking for a fight from the word "here comes the crowd."

At any rate, they just knocked people out of the way and we got the girl to the aid station. After a doctor's examination, we found she was 17 years old, 8 weeks pregnant, unmarried, and high on drugs. She could not take the heat, passed out, and fell. She had to be hospitalized. There goes $18.00 down the drain!

Brent and I hit the floor again. By this time one of the bands had begun to perform. The crowd was going wild. They were pushing together so hard it seemed that even if someone "went down," they could not fall. We asked a more experienced medic how he got anyone out of a crowd like this. He replied, "Hey, man, you'll see them coming over the top. The others will just pass 'em to the sides."

Sure enough! It happened! A young girl came over the top to the side and into the arms of some medics. We just stood there watching. She could not have been over 13 or 14 years old. She had passed out from heat exhaustion.

The paramedics who, by the way, were very good, worked to revive her. Other victims began to come over the top of the kids. Pretty soon we noticed girls who were nude from the waist up sitting on the shoulders of guys in the crowd with out-stretched arms trying to touch their rock gods.

They would say, "Look at mine (breasts). Take mine!"

I could not believe what I was witnessing. I thought, "What is going on! How many parents actually know what happens at one of these!" I looked at Brent and said, "Brent, do you think we're in hell." Brent said, "No, Daddy, as bad as this is, it's still better than hell." My son blew me away with that statement.

By this time **Ozzy Osbourne** was preparing to come on stage. The crowd was getting even more worked up. The heat of the day was upon us in full force. Enough time had elapsed for the kids to get *real "high."* We did not know what to expect. It appeared that things could get dangerous — very dangerous!

We had been informed that the National Society for the Prevention of Cruelty to Animals was going to demand that Ozzy be arrested on stage if he were to hurt any live creature.

You see, this is the man who bit the head off of a live bat and had to undergo a series of rabies shots. This is the man who stomped a young puppy to death on stage at one particular concert. This is the man who was at one time the lead singer for the British "heavy metal" band BLACK SABBATH. This is the man who holds Satanic crosses in his hands when he sings. This is the man who urinates on stage. This man is obviously insane.

We were told, as medics, that if he hurt an animal of any sort, it would incite the biggest riot in the history of this particular place. We were instructed, with all seriousness, to strip off our tee-shirts and head for the nearest exit as fast as we could go.

We were all waiting... the crowd was wound up so tight that I thought at any time it would snap and people would be killed... and *out he came*. THE KIDS WENT CRAZY. It was wild. I have never seen anything like it.

And get this. I was told that this crowd was fairly calm. I thought, "Oh, Lord! What must something *worse* be like?"

Osbourne screamed over the system, "PEOPLE ASKED ME WHAT I WAS GOING TO DO WHEN I GOT HERE!!! I SAID I WAS GOING TO GO F——— ——— CRAZY!!!" With that, the band cranked up and it sounded like Mt. St. Helens erupting. Really, it sounded like an earthquake. You couldn't hear one another talk — and we were at the opposite end of the stadium.

It was during this performance that several bad fights occurred. One young man came to the aid station with a piece of steel sticking in his eye. One came with a compound fracture of the wrist and hand. One young Spanish girl was brought to us in an absolute craze. She had to be strapped to the stretcher. She spit on the doctors, cursed the nurses, and was so violent and strung out that she was taken to the psychiatric ward of a local hospital.

As she was being placed in the ambulance, her boyfriend said, "What are we going to do about him?" He pointed to a corner of the aid station, and there stood a three-year-old Spanish boy with big, brown eyes and a tear-stained face.

We asked who he was and the boyfriend said, "That's her son."

Well, I 'bout couldn't handle that one. We put the child in the ambulance and off they went! We found out later that she had herpes, so we all took alcohol baths with our hands.

The decibel level of the music was so loud that it shook the ground. The crowd was so worked up that they were hurting one another as well as themselves. The medics couldn't get to the ones who needed help; the heat was unbearable; the nudity was rampant; the drugs filled the air and the noses of the youth; the language was so vile it was an outright curse; the aid station was crowded with nice-looking young people who couldn't handle all or a part of the above; and we had only gotten to the second act! It was 8:00 p.m. We had been there since 8:00 a.m., which was not a long time comparatively speaking.

I said, "Brent, have you seen enough?"

"Yes, sir."

"Are you ready to go?"

"Yes, if you are." *I was.*

We made our last rounds, carried a few more to the aid station, told our friends goodbye and pulled out of the staff parking lot.

We went a few blocks, turned a few corners, hit the freeway, and it was as if nothing like what we had just seen was happening close by. Life was going on as usual. Cars were heading to and fro. People were going out with their families to the local ice cream parlors and things were happening with an aura of regularity.

I thought, *"Parents, you just don't know!! You don't know where your children are! Only a few blocks away, locked inside a big stadium, are thousands of young people being manipulated toward ruination by THE god OF ROCK!!"*

I prayed aloud, "DAMN HIM! DAMN THE DEVIL! HE'LL BURN! HE'LL BE CAST INTO THE LAKE OF FIRE! HE'LL GET HIS!! I JUST WISH IT WERE TONIGHT!"

I was horrified at the thought of him taking so many "down the tubes" with him. I thought of the reported deaths at this type of concert. I thought of the hospitalizations...of the overdoses, the pregnancies, the illicit sex, the nudity, the outright punishment of human beings that I had just witnessed. Brent and I rode in silence for some time and reflected.

This concert had cost approximately $350,000. However, the promoters had made tons of money! The groups had gotten rich at the expense of the youth of the area. The concessions had brought in thousands of dollars. The tee-shirt sales exceeded the imagination. The police riot squad was on alert. There was absolutely no modesty inside the concert area. Illegal drugs could be purchased as if one were in a supermarket. The decibel level of the music had damaged the eardrums of many between the stage and the fifty yard line. The messengers of THE god OF ROCK had been allowed to have awesome control over 70,000 kids. People had been hurt, arrested, and hospitalized. Backstage was a carnal gourmet's delight. The average age of the crowd was 15 — 18, and about 65% were middle-class to upper-crust youth. The hard-core Rock fans were allowed to have the run of the mill because of concert experience. The stands were full as well as the floor. The freeway was backed up for miles before and after the concert. A demonic-like Ozzy Osbourne was a hero...a god! Many in tee-shirt security were there because they liked to fight and hurt people. The audience was pressed together to the degree of suffocation. There were big girls, fat girls, pretty girls and nude ones. There were incredible hulks, punks, show-offs, drunks, dopers and some straights. There were those shooting up, and those shot down. There were those who had on the tee-shirts of their gods: Van Halen, ZZ Top, AC⚡DC, Ozzy Osbourne, Ted Nugent, Journey, Foreigner, J. Giles Band, Blue Oyster Cult, etc.

No, I wasn't ready for what I saw. No parent would be. It could *never* be truly described.

"What can we do?" you ask. It is a valid question. What *is* a parent to do? How *can* a youth minister approach this issue without offending the youth in his charge? What *can* a pastor say that would make any difference? My humble opinion? Become informed!

Part of the shock when parents hear this information comes from their admitted ignorance of what the kids are into. You see, what goes on in a Rock concert can only be contained, it cannot be policed. It is a law-free area in which drugs can be used openly with no fear of arrest, and sex is the expected result. The cops will *not* hassle the kids, so they are literally unbridled. Whatever base tendencies are latent on the inside can unashamedly come out.

Why is it that this has been going on for years and parents and churches are still in the dark? Either Satan is plenty shrewd, or we are just plain dumb. Probably a combination of both would be an appropriate answer.

Parents, please do not assume that because you work to clothe and feed your children that they need nothing more. They desperately *need you*. And, if they would be honest, they desperately *want* you.

I praise the Lord for my children, Brent and Holly. They are truly one of God's richest blessings in my life. I want what goes into their minds to be pure and full of truth. I want for them what is real...not the pseudo-glamour that the world flashes at them on a daily basis.

Don't you feel the same way about your children? They are the Lord's heritage to us and His gifts to mold our levels of responsibility.

I have seen families reunited in my lectures concerning THE god OF ROCK. I have seen parents stand in a noncondemning manner alongside their young people, and I have watched them pray and commit themselves to God, and ask for His power to break the bondage that Satan has in their homes. We are fighting an ardent foe!

Be warned! Rock music accepts kids as they are, and takes them to where it wants them to be. This vehicle is being used by God's *arch enemy* to deteriorate and destroy kids on a moment-to-moment basis.

Parents, check out your children's record collection. Ask them to play some of the songs of their favorite groups for you. Get involved...become informed...and then, if necessary, go to war! They are worth it!

If I can help you, write me! I will correspond and send tapes. I care about *who* your children worship. I am praying that family PRIORITIES will be set straight, and we can serve our glorious Lord with fervent zeal.

The contents of this book are designed to aid in informing the concerned.

CHAPTER TWO
THE PRINCE OF THE AIRWAYS

Christians are in a full-scale war, and many do not even kown it. People are being oppressed by spells, hexes, and hypes, and are almost totally ignorant of what is happening. Satan and his hosts have tremendous power. They "hypnotize," dupe, and deceive countless numbers of young people through the vehicle of ROCK MUSIC.

We intend to demonstrate that the lyrics and music of the "heavy metal" world peddle hatred, rebellion, revolution, disregard for parents, rejection of authority, sex, drugs, depression, and the most dreaded killer among youth today — suicide.

It will also be demonstrated that there is a direct connection between ROCK music and witchcraft. Rock will be shown to capitalize on a hard, driving beat, the same of which is used in most forms of white or black magic ceremonies. It is used to addict and hypnotize.

Much of the music which is categorized ROCK is written under the influence of drugs. Drugs are a major message of the lyrics. Of course, we get our English word "pharmacy" from the Greek word "pharmikia" which means sorcery or potion.

The effects of Rock music are devastating. Illicit sex, rebellion, and even death, are only some among many. The results of a heavy beat in idolatrous religions are sexual orgies, fertility rites, nudity, etc.

The results of the beat among the youth of today is much the same.

The approach we will take with the following material will be simple. The purpose is DISCLOSURE on our part, and DISCOVERY on your part. We desire for the book to serve as a Christian's introductory handbook of Rock music. However, the music industry is extremely complex. There are thousand of artists, and many more songs. We certainly cannot cover all of the Rock scene —not even a small part, but we can give a general perspective of the more popular groups that are pushing the message of the "adversary" through the airways.

We must first of all share some background information with regard to our enemy, the Devil. For instance, who is he...where did he come from...is he alone...who is he after...what are his names and weapons?

The Bible teaches that we do not fight against flesh and blood. In other words, we are at war with an unseen enemy. He was, at one time, a being of great beauty and authority. However, because iniquity was found in him, the once-beautiful Lucifer became Satan and fell away from God. Actually he was ousted from his position of authority in heaven. What position? He was heaven's choir director! When he lost his position, he was confined to the lower atmosphere. The fall of Lucifer can be found in Isaiah 14 and Ezekial 28.

In addition to the personal downfall of God's arch enemy, there was the descent of one-third of God's angelic creation. According to Revelation 12:4, when Lucifer rebelled against God, he was not alone. Please bear in mind that God's angelic creation involved myriads and myriads of angels — more than we can possibly imagine!

Ephesians 6:12 passage reveals a FOUR-FOLD breakdown of Satan's army. This is one of the few scriptures which allow us to see what we, as Christians, are really up against. In the following visual aid the breakdown mentioned consits of PRINCIPALITIES — POWERS — RULERS OF DARKNESS — and SPIRITUAL WICKEDNESS IN HIGH PLACES. To be sure, Satan is not alone! He has a highly-orchestrated army under his unquestioned command.

Having an army implies a battle . . . having a battle implies a battleground. One may ask, "Where is the battleground?" The battleground is the lower atmosphere. The earth is the stage for the conflict. (Ezekial 28:17)

In order for you, as the reader, to familiarize yourself with the adversary so as to at least recognize his handiwork in the specific area of Rock music, we have put together the following study outline which will help you examine the POWER . . . CHARACTER . . . and ACTIVITY OF SATAN. Please allow us to use this outline approach, as it is not our purpose or intent to spend a great portion of time dealing with information which may be obtained from books that center around the subject of Satan and demons.

Because it is necessary for us to present some basic information about the enemy, however, we earnestly

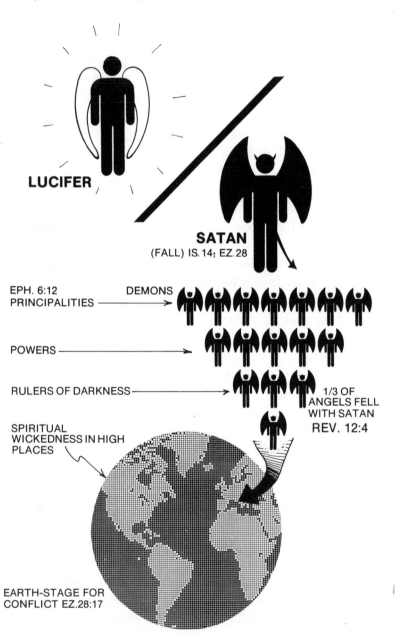

request that you read the outline and look up the scriptures. If you will do this, we can guarantee that you will be assured beyond a shadow of a doubt that the Devil himself has his malignant hands in the Rock music arena.

THE POWER — CHARACTER — ACTIVITY OF SATAN
(A study of his names reveals his nature —
he has over 40 names — here are some:)

I. NAMES REVEALING POWER
    A. *Anointed Cherub* (Ez. 28:14) Highest class
    B. *Prince of this World* (Jn. 12:31) Ruler of Rebels
    C. *God of this Age* (II Cor. 4:4) Counterfeit Philosophy
    D. *Prince of Power of Air* (Eph. 2:2) Atmosphere of Earth
    E. *Prince of Demons* (Matt. 12:24) "Beelzebub" Lord of Flies

(He is a being of great power...not to be slighted)

II. NAMES EXPRESSING CHARACTER
    A. *Lucifer* (Is. 14:12) Light before fall
    B. *Satan* (Zec. 3:1; Rev. 12:9) used 52 times — Adversary; opposer
    C. *Devil* (Lk. 4:2) used 35 times — slanderer
    D. *Evil One* (Jn. 17:15) Intrinsically wicked; spreader of evil

  E. *Old Serpent* (Gen. 3) "Old" — long time;
     serpent — crafty deceptions
  F. *Great Dragon* (Rev. 12:3) Destructive beast
  G. *Destroyer* (Rev. 9:11) Apollyon

  (He is a being of scheming, malignant,
     destructive evil in opposition to God)

III. NAMES MANIFESTING ACTIVITY
  A. *Tempter* (Matt. 4:3) Enticer of men to do evil -
     always active
  B. *Accuser* (Rev. 12:10) Accusations of con-
     demnation — always active
  C. *Deceiver* (Rev. 20:3) False systems — master
     of trickery
  D. *Spirit Working in Sons of Disobedience*
     (Eph. 2:2) Energizes rebellion

  (He is a being of extensive experience,
     knowledge, and ability to transform
     himself in a variety of ways)

Now that you have seen something of who Satan is.. what he is like ... and what he can do, let us go one step further and learn about his accomplices in like manner. Please take the same approach with the following outline concerning demons. Read the outline and look up the scriptures.

THE POWER — CHARACTER — ACTIVITY OF DEMONS

I. DEMONS POSSESS SUPERNATURAL POWER
   A. *Supernatural Intelligence* (Mark 1:24, 34)
   B. *Supernatural Strength*
      in controlling men (Acts 19:16; Mark 5:3)
      in afflicting men (Rev. 9:1-11)
      in working miracles (II Thes. 2:9)
   C. *Supernatural Presence* (Dan. 9.21; 10:10)
      (Lk. 8:30)

   (They are real beings of great power . . .
            not to be slighted)

II. DEMONS EXPRESS EVIL CHARACTER
   A. *In Individuals* (Eph. 2:1-2; I Jn. 2:16)
   B. *In Governments* (Dan. 10:13, 20)
   C. *In World System* (Matt. 12:26; Jn. 12:31;
      Eph. 6:11)

   (They are real beings of scheming,
      malignant, destructive evil)

III. DEMONS MANIFEST OPPOSING ACTIVITY
   A. *Promotion of rebellion* (Rev. 9:20)
   B. *Promotion of idolatry* (Lev. 17:7; Deu. 32:17)
   C. *Promotion of slander*
      Against God (Rom. 3:5-8)
      Against man (Rom. 8:33)
   D. *Promotion of False Teaching* (Col. 2:18-23)

E. *Promotion of Immorality* (Rom. 1:18-32)
F. *Promotion of destruction*
   Truth (II Cor. 4:3)   Body (Lk 13:11)
   Mind (Lk. 8:27)

(They are real beings of extensive experience, knowledge, and ability to transform themselves in a variety of ways)

As you have already noticed in the outline revealing the characteristics of Satan, he is called in Ephesians 2:2, "...the prince of the power of the AIR." the word *AIR* has to do with the stellar atmosphere...the lower air. ITS MEANING YIELDS GREAT INSIGHT AS TO WHY THERE IS SO MUCH POWER BEHIND THE VEHICLE OF ROCK MUSIC. You see, Satan is in charge of what goes over the airways. He is the god of the air: hence, *THE god OF ROCK*.

When a record is played, it is released into the atmosphere. During these latter days, sophisticated technology and the media management of ungodly men has allowed Satan almost free reign in this dimension. He is in varying degrees of control in most stages of airway expression. Consequently, *he* determines what is successful and what is not. Please notice the following diagram which attempts to visualize just how powerful his network really is.

Words are released into the atmosphere through the media...through music. In case you think that words are not powerful, please consider what they

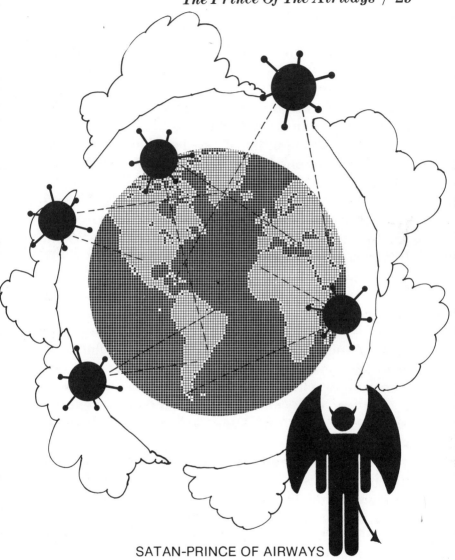

SATAN-PRINCE OF AIRWAYS

NETWORK OF COMMUNICATION

can do. God *created* through the power of the spoken word. (Genesis 1:1-26; Hebrews 11:3) Words can *control...condemn...*and *curse.* James 3:1-12 is a very exact passage of scripture regarding the awesome power of spoken words.

The literal meaning of wisdom has to do with knowledge applied...or better yet, A MESSAGE IMPARTED. The motive of the one delivering the message is the KEY to the results. James 3:13-18 teaches that there are two kinds of WISDOM. Man's wisdom is seen to produce selfishness, fanaticism, bitterness, defensiveness, rebellion, and strife. God's wisdom, or message imparted, produces purity, peace, yieldedness, obedience, joy, and righteousness.

You see, when the heart is right, the message will be in a vehicle of protection. Therefore, when you speak a word, even though it goes out into the atmosphere where Satan lurks, it *cannot* be twisted by the "god of the air" and it will land in the hearer's ear untainted. If your heart is right, it will transfer with power and truth.

Believe me, friends, the message of Rock music is not pure. It is not the TRUTH...it is a LIE. The spoken words are coming through the atmosphere with the intent of destruction. They are Satan's weapons! They are unbelievably devastating! They can actually ruin lives. THE MOTIVE IS TO KILL, and kill they can.

Satan can actually capture a person through the vehicle of Rock music. Let me relate a personal experience that is very relevant to the subject at hand.

It happened in Canada! I was conducting a revival for a church in Saskatoon, Saskatchewan. A young man came to the services one night after having been invited by the pastor's son. He listened intently, and after the message was preached he came to me and requested a time that we might talk together. We arranged an appointment for the following morning.

As he began to share his life story, it became blatantly apparent that he was heavily oppressed by Satanic influence.

He said, "I am a disc jockey in a gay bar!" He then proceeded to tell me that he was gay (homosexual) himself. He told me of nightmares, phobias, voices, and other strange happenings. I knew beyond a doubt that everything he was sharing with me was directly linked to demonic activity.

I listened for a while longer; then I briefly shared how Satan could use the vehicle of Rock music to gain entrance into a person's life and change their thinking...consequently, change their action. I shared how the adversary could purposefully set up strongholds in a person's being.

After this introductory time of explanation on my part, I said, "Lorne, we need to talk to the pastor of this church about your problems! Could you come back tonight?"

He immediately began to shake and sweat profusely. It was very noticeable! I knew what was happening! I spoke outloud, "In the Name of Jesus, I rebuke any demon that would hinder Lorne's decision to return to church tonight!"

He quit shaking...and simply said, "I'll be here!"

I shared the experience with the pastor, and we planned to meet with Lorne after the service. We gathered in the pastor's study, Lorne Reid, Henry Blackaby, and myself.

I asked Lorne to again relate his experiences and how he was earning his living playing "high energy" records for people to get stoned to. As he shared, I silently prayed. The pastor quickly recognized the symptoms, but neither of us were expecting what was about to happen!

We asked Lorne if he wanted to be free from his extreme bondage and his homosexual activity. He said, "YES...YES...OH! YES!!"

We then explained that his root problems probably stemmed from demon activity. His body started to shake and tremble. The pastor and I began to come against the demons. Whenever we spoke the Name of Jesus, Lorne would burst out in wild laughter! His eyes were horrified, but the laughter was uncontrollable! He could not explain it! We could!

It seemed we had been in battle with the powers of darkness for an hour, when we *demanded,"* that Lorne confess, out loud, that Jesus was Lord! He couldn't!

This went on and on. I would speak against the demons and Henry would pray and agree...then Henry would speak against them and I would pray and agree! We both commanded on the authority of the cross, and by the shed blood of our risen Lord

Jesus Christ that the demons release their bondage and allow Lorne to speak the Name of Jesus outloud ... to confess Him as Lord of his (Lorne's) life. However, Lorne *could not* speak the Name of Jesus, no matter how hard he tried. He was terrified! He did not understand what was happening to him!

Finally, with all authority, Henry and I commanded again that the demons loose Lorne's tongue in order that he could speak what he knew to be true in his heart, to say that Jesus was and is really Lord!

At that very moment, Lorne's head went down between his knees and straining unbelievably hard he shouted, "JESUS IS LORD!!! JESUS IS LORD!!! SATAN GET OUT OF ME! JESUS IS MY LORD!!!"

Dear reader, when he yelled those words, his body slammed against the wall so hard that the pastor and I thought he had been knocked unconscious! It was gloriously powerful!

Many other things happened that night as we ministered and counseled with Lorne Reid. However, what really matters is that he was delivered from horrible bondage, set free, and joined to Jesus Christ, the Victor!

Please hear and heed! Music was the main vehicle used for the enemy to gain such a stronghold in Lorne's life. This is his own admission. He freely shares his experience. His company *was* called THE REVOLVING SOUND COMPANY.

He is turning away from his former profession. He is currently seeking to share his new-found freedom! Pray for him. The god of Rock does not let go easily.

Lorne must yield his life to Jesus Christ daily in order to have the necessary power to witness to his former peers who are heavily involved in "high energy" New Wave disco.

Neither Henry Blackaby, Area Missionary for the Northwest Baptist Convention, nor myself will ever forget the night that this young man was delivered from the kingdom of the darkness and translated to the kingdom of the glorious light of God's Son, Jesus Christ!

Thank you, Lord, for your awesome power.

CHAPTER THREE
THE FIVE MAJOR THEMES OF
ROCK MUSIC

The world of Rock music is projecting FIVE MAJOR THEMES. These can be found in the lyrics of songs, in the beat of the music, in the performance of the various groups, and in album cover art. The themes are: 1. SEX; 2. DRUGS; 3. REBELLION; 4. FALSE RELIGION; 5. SATAN. A vast majority of the more popular Rock groups are involved in some kind of Satan-glorifying religion. Many perform before signs and symbols which clearly depict demon worship. As we pursue this line of thinking, we will demonstrate the overwhelming evidence that God has strictly forbidden Christian participation in any of the above activities.

If the five themes are really the basis for the message of Rock music, what *should* be the Christian response? Should the Christian young person perpetrate the message by participation in any manner? Do not take our word for it! Please study the following passages of scripture and decide for yourself.

SEX — THE FIRST MAJOR THEME

The Bible is very clear about this matter. It does *NOT* teach that sex is evil by design. God intended the union of man and woman in a marital relationship to be the ultimate pleasure ... the source of complete fulfillment ... the pure joy of oneness or intimate fellowship. However, in the state of perversion that we see God's beautiful design taking expression in this society, it is definitely one of the adversary's most powerful weapons used against us. It is truly remarkable how Satan can take what was created for our good and turn it around so to destroy lives.

Please notice the following scriptures which relate specifically to the participation of God's people in illicit sex. Of course, the word *fornication*, which is "porneia" in the Greek, is used approximately 40 times in its various forms throughout the Bible. The English word *pornography* came from "porneia." It will be impossible in the space permitted to deal with its total usage. But please keep in mind, only ONE verse is enough to give us God's will in the matter.

> ACTS 15:20: But that we write unto them, that they abstain from pollutions of idols, and from *fornication*, and from things strangled, and from blood.

> ACTS 15:29: That ye abstain from meats offered to idols, and from blood, and from things strangled, and from *fornication:* from which if ye keep yourselves, ye shall do well. Fare ye well.

> ACTS 21:25: As touching the Gentiles which believe, we have written and

concluded that they observe no such thing, save only that they keep themselves from things offered to idols, and from blood, and from strangled, and from *fornication.*

ROMANS 1:28-29, 32: And even as they did not like to retain God in their knowledge, God gave them over to a reprobate mind, to do those things which are not convenient; Being filled with all unrighteousness, *fornication,* wickedness, covetousness, maliciousness; full of envy, murder, debate, deceit, malignity; whisperers, ... Who knowing the judgment of God, that they which commit such things are worthy of death, not only do the same, but have pleasure in them that do them.

I CORINTHIANS 6:13: Meats for the belly, and the belly for meats: but God shall destroy both it and them. Now the body is not for *fornication,* but for the Lord; and the Lord for the body.

I CORINTHIANS 6:18: Flee *fornication.* Every sin that a man doeth is without the body; but he that committeth *fornication* sinneth against his own body.

GALATIANS 5:19: Now the works of the flesh are manifest, which are these;

Adultery, fornication, uncleanness, lasciviousness.

REVELATION 18:3: For all nations have drunk of the wine of the wrath of her *fornication,* and the kings of the earth have committed *fornication* with her, and the merchants of the earth are waxed rich through the abundance of her delicacies.

There are so many explicit verses that teach that we, as Christians, are NOT to be a part of fornication. Fornicators will not inherit the kingdom of God. (I Cor. 6:9)

Being very realistic, the abuse of God's planned design is one of the more dangerous messages of Rock. Our society has been so deadened and dulled by the bombardment of Satan's perversion that many do not even consider immorality a vital issue. Men and women, made in the image of God, are being exploited and even ruined by promiscuous thinking in this area. When a young girl loses her virginity because of listening to music that lowers her basic inhibitions, some snicker and think it is cute. Dear friends, God does *not* think that at all!! There will be a payday someday! You see, a girl can only give herself the first time ONE time! It is no "cute" thing when she slips and falls.

The mark of fallen society is seen in its views on sexuality. Many people actually seem to be "turned on" by the message of immorality in the music of today. One of the more popular albums on the scene is named "Hi Infidelity." When we look at lyrics later on, we will certainly be able to more clearly perceive what is going on.

Another thing . . . where did our young people get the idea that homosexuality or bisexuality are alternate lifestyles instead of sin? Where did they get the concept that people should experiment with sex in all forms? How *did* they begin to think so loosely about what was intended to be the greatest pleasure that a man and a woman could have within the design structure of God?

The tremendous influence of a role model can never be measured. The only way one can ever know how powerful the pressure is would be to examine the results. Of course, on a very small scale it is easy to spot the parent model in the child. It is also quite simple to spot the professor model in the student. However, today's major trend setters in the realms of style and morality are from the entertainment world.

Rock performers probably have a greater influence on the value system of teenagers than we could ever imagine. It should not shock anyone, who has not had his head in the sand, that the world of Rock portrays homosexuality as the cultural reflection that it is. Gays are coming "out of the closet" in all areas of society. Rock musicians seem to be capitalizing on this, and spreading the movement with hellish fury.

Some of the better-known rock stars who are gay are Lou Reed and David Bowie. Reed is a former member of The Velvet Undergound (the name speaks for itself). Reed is seen with mascara, rouge, panty hose, and high heels on the cover of the album "Transformer." He sings songs like "Makeup," "Good Night, Ladies," and others that describe the loneliness of the homosexual.

David Bowie usually appears wearing women's clothing and makeup. Some have said that his antics are only "hype." Not so! He boasts of being bisexual in interviews. His wife is an admitted lesbian. He simulates sex acts with other males while performing. He sings songs such as "Queen Bitch" (about a homosexual) and performs with orange hair, laced high heel boots, and female movements.

Other female impersonators and gay recording artists include Alice Cooper, who for some time has been coming on stage wearing women's clothing and makeup. Todd Rudgren performs wearing multicolored shoulder-length hair (wigs) and struts onstage sporting corsets and black lingerie. Brain Eno and Iggy Pop are also on the bandwagon. Wayne County, an absurd artist, has made wild accusations about Jesus Christ being gay. He sings songs like, "It Takes a Man Like Me to Love a Woman Like Me." Mick Jagger has certainly not remained silent about his bisexual leanings. One of his recent girlfriends said that Mick was a very sexy man when he was not with another man! Elton John has professed his bisexuality to the top of his vocal chords. Queen derived their name from a drag overtone of the word *GAY*.

The number of gay artists in the Rock music scene can only be measured by the effect that the industry has upon society. And what is the result of this effect? *Devastating* to say the least! The songs advocating homosexuality include "MakeUp," "Queen Bitch," "Gay and Proud," "Women Loving Women," "All the Girls Love Alice," "Let My People Be," "Glad to be Gay," etc. These only condition society to accept on the surface what has been underground for some time.

The New Wave and Punk groups constantly expose their bisexual leanings in their dress, music, and mannerisms. They are too numerous to mention. A few would include Adam and The Ants, Toyah Wilson, Blondie, The Police, Prince, Duran Duran, Human League, and so many others it is not worth the time or the space. To be sure, homosexuality and bisexuality have burst upon the scene with the help of Rock stars of the same persuasion. If one is not at least "bi," he is nothing in the world of "metal" music. Things are definitely out of control.

Well, what about the Christian young person? What does the Bible say about this issue? Should a man marry a man? Should a person have sexual affairs with both sexes? Is it all right to experiment with a person of the same sex...especially if these are your leanings or feelings? In the following pages, we will simply mention some passages of scripture and you be the judge!!

For a truth, our States are beginning to liberalize their sexual activity laws. Most of the laws concerning sexual perversion are being reformed across the country in favor of homosexuals and their counterpart. Why? This author recently heard some alarming news. There is a community of gays in the Houston, Texas, area numbering over 300,000. The voter turnout for the area was 92%. This is opposed to a 12% turnout in the surrounding neighborhoods. Throughout America today the influence of homosexuals is being more widely felt than ever before. Major denominations are politely defending the rights and privileges of this group. Federal and state legislators and leaders in high places are debating the pro-gay proposals, and will probably soon endorse a new bill that will give the homosexual more freedom which will undoubtedly affect this nation's destiny. In some current court cases gays are seeking to adopt children!

There are diverse interpretations about what God says about this perversion. However, upon a surface glance, one can clearly see that the Old Testament and the New Testament condemn its practice. In Leviticus 18:22 and 20:13, homosexuality was punishable by death. The book of Romans describes it as the culminating sexual perversion of man's apostasy and hostility towards God. In other words, Romans 1 portrays the sin as being at war with God.

Just before the destruction of Sodom, homosexuals desired to besiege the house of Lot and attempted to seduce two angels sent from God. This account is found in Genesis 19. We are witnessing a similar stream of immorality in this country and around the world. It seemed to be gradual at first, but has now melted into a mighty rushing river. Homosexuals and bisexuals are serving on the staffs of churches...as postmasters...as printers...as grocery store clerks...as school teachers...as oil executives...as attorneys...as judges...as preachers...etc., etc. You name it, and there is a homosexual involved in it.

Of course, leave it to the deep-seated perversion of the Rock music industry to bring this absurdity to the forefront. These deranged musicians are not only trendsetters, but they also know how to get on a publicity bandwagon. They can find out, with devilish knack, how to turn up at the right place at the right time.

Statistics reveal that the number of homosexuals in this country is rapidly approaching the ten percent mark. This means that there are twenty million or more, and the number is spreading like a fire-storm on the Nevada desert. Please realize, this figure only represents the number of PROFESSING GAYS. Only God knows how many there really are! "Closet gays" (those who practice homosexuality or bisexuality and do not tell anyone due to social pressure or their position) are everywhere.

II Timothy 3:1-5 tells us that men will be lovers of themselves in the last days. I Corinthians 6:9 says that no one who practices this sin will have a part in the Kingdom of God. R.J. Rushdonny, in this work *The Institute of Biblical Law* says, "It is customary among humanists to regard homosexuality as a natural act which is a phase in the erotic development of man. The Biblical view is that it is an act against God and therefore against nature."

Dear friends, may we remind you that according to Hosea 4:14, when a person reaches a certain level of moral depravity, punishment ceases to be personal and becomes national. We are fast approaching this time. How did we come to this point? How could a country as great as this climb aboard the DOWNBOUND TRAIN without even knowing the destination? ROCK MUSIC SPREAD THE NEWS! ROCK MUSICIANS CALLED THEIR FORCES OUT OF THEIR COFFINS!! THE GOD OF ROCK IS USING HIS MESSENGERS TO ROUND UP THE PASSENGERS, AND BOARD THE TRAIN!! The young person who "digs" the music of an artist and finds that his god is a homosexual is likely to experiment with latent tendencies or even advocate the practice.

Can our young people, whom we have taught proper truths about perversions, endure after hearing daily that homosexuality is all right. And where would they repetitiously hear this? FROM THEIR FAVORITE ROCK GROUPS! FROM THEIR ROCK IDOLS!! We need to be awakened! We need, as parents, to become aware of this powerful onslaught. Christian young person, you must become informed about this problem and learn to speak from a Biblical standpoint what you know to be true. We've not much time to turn around.

DRUGS — THE SECOND MAJOR THEME

Again, we must remind the readers that we are extremely limited on space and will not be able to present an in-depth look into the realm of drug abuse. It is not our purpose. We are seeking to demonstrate that it is BIBLICALLY wrong to be involved with drugs in an abusive manner. It is strictly prohibited by God to seek extra-biblical revelation through drug-induced means. Here again, this is one of the major themes of Rock music. Musicians use drugs to write lyrics that inspire millions of people to use drugs as well.

What should the Christian young person do when he hears a lyric in the music that advises him to experiment or escape through the use of drugs? What does the Bible teach? There are many verses that address this problem; but remember, it only takes one.

As we saw in our survey of the last theme, the word translated *fornication* was the Greek word *porneia*. In our scan of the drug theme, the Greek word *pharmakia* is translated *sorcery*. As has previously been mentioned, we get out English word *pharmacy* (drug house) from the Greek word *pharmakia*. Does the Bible refer to sorcery in relationship to drugs? YES! Please notice:

REVELATION 9:21: Neither repented they of their murders, nor of their *sorceries*, nor of their fornication, nor of their thefts.

REVELATION 18:23: And the light of a candle shall shine no more at all in thee; and the voice of the bridegroom and of the bride shall be heard no more at all in thee: for thy merchants were the great men of the earth; for by the *sorceries* were all nations deceived.

REVELATION 21:8: But the fearful, and unbelieving, and the abominable, and murderers, and whoremongers, and *sorcerers*, and idolaters, and all liars, shall have their part in the lake which burneth with fire and brimstone: which is the second death.

REVELATION 22:15: For without are dogs, and *sorcerers*, and whoremongers, and murderers, and idolaters, and whosoever loveth and maketh a lie.

GALATIONS 5:19-20: Now the works of the flesh are manifest, which are these; adultery, fornication, uncleanness, lasciviousness, idolatry, *witchcraft*, hatred, variance, emulations, wrath, strife, seditions, heresies.

A sorcerer is identified in the scripture as one who is devoted to the magical arts, especially one who uses drugs, potions, spells, enchantments, or incantations. The term *pharmakia* primarily signifies the use of medicine, drugs, spells, poisoning, or witchcraft.

According to Isaiah 47:9-12, nations that are totally dependent upon the protection of Satan through the use of sorcery will be utterly destroyed. We are almost there!

In sorcery, the use of drugs was generally accompanied by appeals to occult powers. This is so prevalent in Rock music that it is absolutely frightening. A very high percentage of musicians of the present use drugs and advocate that others do the same. Satan is worshipped during performances, and prayed to during sessions. Little wonder! He is in control of the success of whatever goes over the airways. HE IS THE god OF ROCK.

As has previously been mentioned, I have been personally present when young people by the scores were brought into first aid stations during Rock concerts with *drug-related* illnesses. I have seen auditoriums filled with youth and the sweet smell of marijuana to the extent that the police could only surround the concert hall from the outside and *contain* the madness. I have driven ambulances when numerous automobile accidents involving young people occurred in a short span of time immediately following a Rock concert. I am amazed at the awesome power of the enemy in situations like this.

Deuteronomy 18:10-11 is an outright prohibition against the use of drugs for the purpose of seeing or feeling another dimension. Whether it is admitted or not, this is what people who use drugs to abuse are seeking to do. They desire to be in another world. They cannot seem to handle the present one, or simply do not want to. Please notice, "There shall not be found among you any one that maketh his son or his daughter to pass through the fire, or that useth divination, or an observer of times, or an enchanter, or a witch, or a charmer, or a consulter with familiar spirits, or a wizard, or a necromancer." Deut. 18:10-11.

IT WOULD LITERALLY ASTOUND YOU, dear reader, if you knew all of the lyrics of the various acceptable groups that our youth listen to. There is not much that would pass the test of Deuteronomy 18:10-11.

Following are only several examples of may drug-related deaths of the stars of Rock:

Tommy Bolin - Deep Purple
Tim Buckley
Nick Drake
Tim Hardin
Jimi Hendrix
Gregory Herbert - Blood, Sweat and Tears
Janis Joplin
Frankie Lymon
Robbie McIntosh - Average White Band
Keith Moon - The Who
Gram Parsons
Elvis Presley
Sid Vicious - The Sex Pistols
Danny Whitten - Crazy Horse
Alan Wilson - Canned Heat
Jim Morrison - Doors
Duane Allman - The Allman Brothers (Motorcycle)
Barry Oakley - The Allman Brothers

(Motorcycle)
   and others too numerous to mention

Drug-related arrests involve hundreds of groups
and stars. Keith Richards, Mick Jagger, Paul
McCartney, Brian Jones, John Lennon, Janis Joplin,
The Grateful Dead, Jerry Garcia, to name only a
few.

Many Rock stars have committed suicide. No one
knows what actually caused their deaths, but close
friends speculate that drugs, causing deep
depression, added to their fateful decisions.
However, anyone who knows the enemy very well
knows that he is bent on destroying even those who
worship him. Destroy he can...destroy he
will...and destroy he does.

Should the Christian young person be in any way
involved in the use of drugs — which are directly
related to witchcraft? ABSOLUTELY NOT!!

REBELLION — THE THIRD MAJOR THEME

A blatant denial of authority on all levels is directly
and forcefully presented by the messengers of Rock.
Not only is this seen in the lyrics of the songs, but the
most penetrating power of the message of rebellion
is lived out in the examples of the musicians
themselves. Most Rock musicians are treated like
gods; consequently, some actually believe they are. If
you know anything about them, you can almost hear
the words scream out, "HEY, TEACHER...LEAVE

THEM KIDS ALONNNNE!" (Lyrics from a very popular song.)

Rock stars are noted for being the most destructive of all traveling people. They have been banned from motels and hotels all over the world. They have been fined, sued, evicted, and even shot. They thumb their noses at all forms of authority. They curse, vomit, spit, and other gross types of excretion anywhere they desire...ANYWHERE! This example is caught, not taught. That is why it is so dangerous. Whatever these calculating hypesters do becomes the current trend. The protest songs of Rock music are much too numerous to mention. There are thousands. (Discussed in a following section.)

What should be the Christian's response to rebellion? Does the Bible teach us how God actually perceives a rebel...a person who defies authority? Of course, Satan is the ARCH REBEL. Therefore, anyone who is under his dominion falls into the same category.

The word *rebellion* is used over 90 times in the Old Testament alone. The word in its various forms means: to turn aside; to make bitter; to transgress; to provoke.

Please examine the following scriptures keeping in mind that only one would be enough to instruct the Christian to refrain from rebellion.

NUMBERS 14:9: Only *rebel* not ye against the Lord, neither fear ye the people of the land; for they are bread for us: their defense is departed from them, and the Lord is with us: fear them not.

JOSHUA 22:19: Notwithstanding, if the land of your possession be unclean, then pass ye over unto the land of the possession of the Lord, wherein the Lord's tabernacle dwelleth, and take possession among us: but *rebel* not against the Lord, nor *rebel* against us, in building you an altar beside the altar of the Lord our God.

PSALM: 5:10: Destroy thou them, O God; let them fall by their own counsels; cast them out in the multitude of their transgressions; for they have *rebelled* against thee.

ISAIAH 1:20: But if ye refuse and *rebel*, ye shall be devoured with the sword: for the mouth of the Lord hath spoken it.

I SAMUEL 15:23: For *rebellion* is as the sin of witchcraft, and stubbornness is as iniquity and idolatry. Because thou hast rejected the word of the Lord, he hath also rejected thee from being king.

PROVERBS 17:11: An evil man seeketh only *rebellion*: therefore a cruel messenger shall be sent against him.

> PSALM 66:7: He ruleth by his power for ever; his eyes behold the nations: let not the *rebellious* exalt themselves. Selah.

> ISAIAH 30:1: Woe to the *rebellious* children, saith the Lord, that take counsel, but not of me; and that cover with a covering, but not of my spirit, that they may add sin to sin.

After studying this word and thinking about the message of rebellion in the vehicle of Rock music, I am amazed that we have even survived the attack at all. This is assuming that we *have* survived. It is no wonder, however, that our youth are deadened and dulled to spiritual things. It certainly explains why they can't listen to the Word of God for any length of time. It gives crystal-clear insight as to the breakdown of authority in our nation — especially in our schools.

I am familiar with a school superintendent who is the head of a most ungodly school system. In doing research for this book, I learned one of the reasons why. The entire upstairs of his house, where his children live, is plastered with "heavy metal" Rock albums. In case one might think this irrelevant, please understand that the lyrics of this music attack the mind ... even subliminally. This very definitely shows up in the decision-making process of the schools under his administration.

Rebellion is extremely dangerous! An account must be given to God by everyone who rebels and all who advocate it. And, may I sadly say...God's judgment will be very great. Christian, do *not* rebel against your Lord.

FALSE RELIGION — THE FOURTH MAJOR THEME

False religions of all sorts are believed and preached through the Rock message. This is certainly a major theme. Most of the religions are of Eastern origin, and came into this country on the wings of superstars like the Beatles, Jimi Hendrix, Seals and Croft, and countless others.

It seems that if groups do not have a "god" of some sort to project, they simply find one. There are so many idols presented in the symbolism on album covers that a fairly exhaustive study of FALSE RELIGIONS in America could be constructed from these alone.

What does the Bible teach about worshipping, or even bowing to false gods (idols)? Is the Christian to "eat at the table of idols?" What should be the response of the Christian young person to the presentation of a "god" other than the God of the Bible?

Please consider the following verses:

LEVITICUS 19:4: Turn ye not unto idols, nor make to yourselves molten gods: I am the Lord your God.

LEVITICUS 26:1: Ye shall make you no idols nor graven image, neither rear you up a standing image, neither shall ye set up any image of stone in your land, to bow down unto it: for I am the Lord your God.

ISAIAH 2:18: And the idols he shall utterly abolish.

II CHRONICLES 24:18: And they left the house of the Lord God of their fathers, and served groves and idols: and wrath came upon Judah and Jerusalem for this their trespass.

HOSEA 14:8: Ephraim shall say, What have I to do any more with idols? I have heard him, and observed him: I am like a green fir tree. From me is thy fruit found.

MICAH 1:7: And all the graven images thereof shall be beaten to pieces, and all the hires thereof shall be burned with the fire, and the idols therof will I lay desolate: for she gathered it of the hire of an harlot, and they shall return to the hire of an harlot.

ACTS 15:20: But that we write unto them, that they abstain from pollutions of idols, and from fornication, and from things strangled and from blood.

ROMANS 2:22: Thou that sayest a man should not commit adultery, dost thou commit adultery? Thou that abhorrest idols, dost thou commit sacrilege?

II CORINTHIANS 6:16: And what agreement hath the temple of God with idols? For ye are the temple of the living God; as God hath said, I will dwell in them, and walk in them; and I will be their God, and they shall be my people.

I JOHN 5:21: Little children, keep yourselves from idols. Amen.

REVELATION 9:20: And the rest of the men which were not killed by these plagues yet repented not of the works of their hands, that they should not workship devils, and idols of gold, and silver, and brass, and stone, and of wood: which neither can see, nor hear, nor walk.

Idolaters will not have inheritance in the kingdom of God. God will put down idolatrous nations and idolatrous people. The word translated idols is used approximately 130 times in both Testaments. Idolatry, and the worship that goes with this horrible distraction, is an abomination to God. From the Biblical point of view, He strictly forbids it. History records nations crumbling because of this heinous sin.

The Christian has no alternatives. God has made it very explicit in Exodus 20:3-5. Please pay close attention to the following scripture. "Thou shalt have no other gods before me. Thou shalt not make unto thee any graven image, or any likeness ... Thou shalt not bow down thyself to them, nor serve them; for I the Lord the God am a jealous God, visiting the iniquity of the fathers upon the children unto the third and fourth generation of them that hate me."

Jesus taught in Matthew 4, as He was undergoing the temptation experience, that we must worship the Lord our God and Him ONLY should we serve.

There is no doubt that the Bible teaches quite specifically that the Christian should not be involved in anything that perpetrates the message of FALSE RELIGIONS.

SATAN — THE FIFTH MAJOR THEME

The final major theme of Rock music is the outright worship of Satan himself. This is where the Devil comes out into the open, and this is what he has wanted all along. He told Jesus that He could have anything the world had to offer if He (Jesus) would only bow down and worship him. This is his desire, plan, and purpose.

There are numerous groups on the Rock scene who make "no bones" about why they are successful. They know that their success is directly attributed to *THE god OF ROCK* ... Satan. And to obtain that success, they have sold their souls. In fact, there is one group, namely **BLACK SABBATH**, who recorded an album entitled "We Have Sold Our Soul to Rock'n Roll."

You see, the reason that the messengers of Rock must "sell out" to Satan in order to be successful, is the awesome truth that he *is* in control of the airways. In order to have a best-selling record, there must be airplay...conversely, in order to have the airplay, there must be a best-selling record. This circle is very tight. There are musicians the world over who are trying to "crack the circle," so to speak. How do they do it? They must dedicate their records to Satan. He is in charge of the circle.

This is the reason numerous groups have adopted various Satanic symbols as their logos. Satanic crosses, hexagrams, pentagrams, and other demonic symbols literally permeate the art and advertising.

Should the Christian young person become involved with anything that places Satan, God's arch enemy, in the forefront? Are there consequences in the life of a Christian who pays no heed to the scripture which addresses this practice? Does scripture pertain to this issue? Is ignorance an excuse?

God does not take our succumbing to this temptation lightly. Please notice!

> MATTHEW 4:10: Then saith Jesus unto him, Get thee hence, Satan; for it is written, Thou shalt worship the Lord thy God, and him only shalt thou serve.

> MATTHEW 16:23: But he turned, and said
> unto Peter, Get thee behind me, Satan: thou
> art an offence unto me: for thou savourest
> not the things that be of God, but those that
> be of men.

So many are the Biblical references to this malignant being that we cannot do the prohibitions justice by naming only a few. So, please refer to the previous outline which examines his character and illumines the danger of our involvement with him in any matter.

There is much to be said about keeping ourselves from the very *appearance* of evil. However, we must remember that Satan *IS* evil. There is nothing he does that is good. Whenever he is worshipped, the inevitable result is destruction now and destruction forever. Be very careful, and be very sure that God will rest His judgment upon those who follow His enemy.

These are the FIVE MAJOR THEMES of Rock music. As you can see, they do NOT glorify our Lord. Many say, "Well, it doesn't seem so bad to me...it's only music...I never listen to the lyrics anyway." Excuses! Excuses! Grow up to what is going on in the spiritual realm concerning this type of music. It is dangerous! It is deadly; addictive; and subconsciously devastating. It can produce hostility, fatigue, panic, indigestion, and hypertension. It is not a harmless pastime...it is said to be more harmful than heroin. It is negative and destructive. It is not a symptom, but probably an actual cause for many of our country's problems. It has its roots in Africa, South America and India. These cultures are steeped in voodoo rituals, witchcraft of all sorts, animism, sexual orgies in the worship of deities, human sacrifice, and demon worship. Oh yes...it should be dealt with!!! Christians must wake up to the awesome power of this, the enemy's greatest weapon of our time. The youth affected by the message of Rock music today will be the leaders of our nation ten years from now. This is a very sobering thought. Nevertheless, inevitably the truth, if the Lord tarries.

CHAPTER FOUR
THE SUBLIMINAL ATTACK ON THE MIND

Do the messages of Rock music toy with the mind? Are there hidden lyrics, that if played backward reveal an evil message? Are the messengers of Rock messing with the minds of their listeners, and they, the listeners, do not even know it? Yes...very definitely!

The technique of "backmasking," or backward masking falls into the category of subliminal persuasion which is as close to being mind controlled as people can be without becoming consciously aware that they are being directed by an outside force. A subliminal message is a message that is below a discernable level. The conscious mind picks up one message...the subconscious mind picks up another.

The mind works much like a computer. It is very precise with the information it stores...and it stores everything. Of course, one may not be able to recall certain things, but if data has ever been received by the empirical sense system, it is stored.

There has been much scoffing, from the defenders of Rock, at the notion that the subconcious mind can understand lyrics played backward. However, subliminal communications experts have clinically proven that the mind can decipher the garble. One particular organization in Louisiana has yielded information stating the positive uses of subliminal messages for therapy patients and weight control. Their experience demonstrates that the brain has "uncanny" abilities to decode messages that are played backward. In fact, the above-mentioned organization holds a patent on a device called a "subliminal processor." This is a very efficient, and sophisticated piece of equipment. However, one can do backward masking with parts that can be purchased at Radio Shack.

The process is fairly simple. One records the purposed message, then plays it backward. After listening to the backward message there needs to be found an innocuous message that sounds similar to the backward message to be played forward. Or, one can simply reverse the word forms. With the equipment found in many of the more elite studios, this would be a very simple task.

Subliminal messages, for the purpose of advertising, are against the law. However, the use of this approach to the mind is very much open in the music industry. There has been nothing to prevent it thus far.

Mick Jagger of the Rolling Stones said in a recent interview, "We've had their bodies...now, we want their minds." Jagger is called the "Lucifer of Rock." (More later.)

The late Jimi Hendrix once said, "Music is a spiritual thing. You can hypnotize people with music and when they get at their weakest point you can preach into their subconscious minds what you want to say."

Grand Nash says, "Rock music is the most popular method of conditioning the way people think."

It could be said that music is the single most powerful instrument known among the methods of affecting the thinking processes. As has already been stated, a person who has been in the dimension of Rock music for even a short period of time has in his subconscious an influence that will wage war against the hearing and doing of the Word of God.

There is no doubt that our society is accepting things that even a few short years ago we would not have accepted. Why? We have been brainwashed! Our youth think hardly anything about things that horrify their parents. They have become deadened to God's standards; consequently, their parents have compromised in order to maintain some peace in the home.

Young people are saying to their authorities, "Aw! Everyone is doing that!" Where did they get that idea? Where did they begin to think that promiscuous sex is all right? Where did they get the idea that there is nothing harmful about drug abuse? How could they be so dull to the danger of rebellion against their parents, their teachers, their government, and God? Who told them that it was all right to worship idols. After all, they aren't real, so what's the big deal? Where could they have possibly gotten their faulty thinking about Satan? LISTEN CAREFULLY! If they didn't get it directly from their parents, and if they didn't hear it directly from their other authorities, and no one that you can think of has been outwardly teaching these errors, that leaves only one place. THE MEDIA!!!! Rock music is the greatest teacher of false doctrine ever devised by the destroyer. Herein lies the FAULTY CLASSROOM, and most youth do not even know that they are being deceived.

In his book, *The Big Beat*, Frank Garlock states on page 11: "The disciples of chaos and disorder could not have found a more perfect vehicle to promote and instill their ideas and philosophies in a generation of young people. The two countries where Rock 'n Roll is most popular, the United States and England, have not only the highest juvenile deliquency rates in the world but also the greatest increase in juvenile crime rate, in illegitimate birth rate, in over-all crime rate, and the worst suicide rate in the world. After his daughter's death in 1969, Art Linkletter blamed 'secret messages' in Rock music lyrics for encouraging young people to take part in the growing problem of drug abuse."

There has definitely been a subliminal attack on the mind through the vehicle of Rock music. It has been a secretive yet systematic move of the adversary. Although Rock is extremely dangerous, it is thought to be harmless, therefore, it does its damage unchallenged. When are we Christians going to see this and do something about it?

Some of the many groups that use the technique of "backward masking" are "THE BEATLES, LED ZEPPELIN, BLACK OAK ARKANSAS, QUEEN, BLACK SABBATH, ELECTRIC LIGHT ORCHES-

TRA, SANTANA, KISS, BLUE OYSTER CULT, THE ROLLING STONES, and others. Many messages, we are sure, are yet undetected.

To give a very brief idea of what is being said through the subliminal approach, notice the following excerpts.

In the songs "Stairway to Heaven" from the Led Zeppelin album of the same name the backward message of one verse says, "I will sing because I live with Satan...my sweet Satan, the one who will be the sad one who makes me sad, whose power is Satan."

In the song "The Day Electricity Came to Arkansas," the group Black Oak Arkansas uses backmasking to say "Satan, Satan, Satan, he is god, he is god, he is god."

In Queen's song, "Another One Bites the Dust," the words of the title are repeated several times at the end of the song. Played backward, one will hear, "Decide to smoke marijuana...decide to smoke marijuana."

With lyrics that advocate godlessness both frontward and backward...sounds played at such a high decibel level as to cause deafness...a strong, driving, throbbing beat which releases undisguised and uncontrolled impulses in the listener, the phenomenon of Rock music could be the most devastating force of all times.

CHAPTER FIVE
THE MESSENGERS AND THEIR MESSAGE

The preceding background information has been strictly for the purpose of familiarizing the reader with the sordid scene of the Rock music world. There has certainly not been the space to have given each of these areas their just examination. However, as we have said, the purpose of the book is to present the serious Christian something in hand for reference concerning the messengers of *THE god OF ROCK*. Following is a description of approximately 85 Rock music groups and single performers. We will attempt to look briefly at the members of the group, where they got their name, when they were formed, what they stand for, some of their songs, and the artwork on their album covers. The rating code relates to the five major themes. (SE-Sex; D-Drugs; R-Rebellion; FR-False Religions; SA-Satan)

AC⚡DC (SE, D, R, SA)

The group AC⚡DC is Australian and has yet to do anything but play very loudly. They actually scream their petty lyrics. AC⚡DC is considered a "heavy metal" band and centers around the whiplash riffing of guitarists Angus and Malcomb Young.

The group's lead singer, Bon Scott, died February 19, 1980, of alcohol poisoning.

The hyphen between the AC and DC is a Satanic S.

Their name stands for bisexuality.

The members of AC⚡DC are hard-livers extraordinaire. The group was formed in the mid-'70's and has risen to the top of the "heavy metal" world because of the stadium Rock phenomonon in this country.

The group has recorded songs entitled "Evil Walk," "Spellbound," "Inject the Venom," and "Snowballed." The artwork on their album covers allows one to know what the group stands for at a glance. For example, the cover of the "If You Want Blood You've Got It" has a member of the group with the neck of a guitar rammed through his stomach and blood splattered over the rest of the band and stage. On the cover of the album "Highway To Hell" there are pentagrams (major symbol of witchcraft) around the necks of members and the horns of Satan growing out of the head of the lead singer. The cover of "Powerage" has a member of the group wired like a robot and being shortcircuited. Another album title is "Dirty Deeds Done Cheap." "Back in Black" has been on the charts in this country for some time at this writing.

AC⚡DC is a group of high-amp boogie men who have been sowing seeds of destruction on the road for several years. Stop sowing, guys—the seeds are getting out of control.

ADAM AND THE ANTS (SE, D, R)

Adam Ant is part of the fairly recent "PUNK" and "NEW WAVE" movement. This trend in music has its roots in Great Britain, but, unfortunately, has migrated to the United States through groups such as the Ants.

"Punk," as it is rightfully called, is nothing but an outburst of garbled and unintelligible lyrics forcefully thrust to a drunken, surly, unruly mob of leather-bound, mohawk-headed kids. "Punk," or "New Wave," is pitiful. It is very sordid and very dirty. The more shocking the music, and the filthier the performers, the more successful they become. Such is the case with Adam and the Ants.

This group sets the pace for the "Punk" scene, as they are seen wearing the clothes and makeup of women. On the cover of their album "Prince Charming" all of the members of the group dress as women. They have recorded songs such as "The Third Adam," which is a sacreligious take-off on the second Adam (I Cor. 15:45) who is Chirst. Adam, in the song "Animals and Men," wrote, "War is the world's only hygiene."

Adam is *not* one of the world's great minds, to say the least. However, this group influences countless numbers of young people. Ants are everywhere . . . They've come to the world's picnic.

AEROSMITH (SE, D, FR, SA)

This no-frills Rock band came together in the summer of 1970 as a $30.00-a-night band to entertain locals in the Boston area. For several years they were classed as Rolling Stones sound-alikes, until a very strong regional following rose to cult status. The group was fairly confined to the New England area until the release of their second album "Get Your Wings," which extended them to nationwide acceptance through extensive touring.

Aerosmith cover art projects the basic statement of the group. The cover of the album entitled "Aerosmith" is a *winged globe*. The winged globe is the symbol of the Egyptian sun god Ra. The cover of "Get Your Wings" pictures bat wings. The cover of "Toys in the Attic" is a young child crawling into a seeming picture of an attic full of toys which appear as demonic depictions.

Although they *do* have wings, they will never soar the heavenlies in their condition!

ALLMAN BROTHERS BAND (SE, D)

The Allman Brothers Band was formed in 1969 to be the centerpiece of a new record label. The group was built around the mournful blues style of Greg Allman and the obvious guitar ability of brother Duane Allman. The band's music is a complex blend of blues, rhythm and blues, bluegrass, country, and Southern bar boogie.

Duane Allman was killed in a motorcycle accident, reportedly drug related, in Macon, Georgia, on October 29, 1971. One year later bassist Barry Oakley was killed in the exact same manner in approximately the same spot as Duane. They are buried side by side in the Rose Hill Cemetery in

Macon, Georgia. This is certainly more than coincidental.

In 1974 Greg Allman launched his own career. He began heavy involvement with heroin which eventually led to the breakup of the group and a vicious drug scandal. They have since reformed, to a certain extent, but remain a seed-bed for personal disaster. The album "Brothers of the Road" has a giant mushroom on the cover depicting drugs. The blues are making us blue . . . mass depression!

BACHMAN TURNER OVERDRIVE (FR)

This classic-formula rock band was formed in 1972 by Randy Bachman after he left the successful group, Guess Who. The BTO soon supplanted the Guess Who as Canada's top rock group. Other than being a cash-register boogie band with late '70 flair, the members of BTO are Rock's bestknown Mormons. No alcohol, dope, tea, coffee, or immorality...just pure, clean heresy. The meaning of a "classic formula" band is that they follow the formula explicitly. Of course, the formula is not hard: Keep it simple and play REAL loud.

Their single "You Ain't Seen Nothing Yet" made serious inroads into the American teenybopper market with characteristically bombastic lyrics. Do not be deceived. To Christianity, Mormanism is a cult.

BAD COMPANY (SE, D, R, SA)

This British-born Rock group was formed in late 1973 as a spin-off of the less successful band, Free. Bad Company is deeply involved with the Led Zeppelin organization. This gives insight into their very remarkable success as a concert draw. Satan is glorified by anything that Led Zeppelin (an occultish Rock group) touches.

Although their slam-bam Rock tactics are causing them to achieve success, their message is clearly seen in the lyrics of the hit singles "Feel Like Making Love," "Can't Get Enough," and "Young Blood."

The thrust of Bad Company is their promotion of illicit sex. If you play Bad Company...you are definitely in bad company!

BEATLES (SE, D, R, FR, SA)

Of all of the groups that have and will be mentioned in this glossary, more could be said about the Beatles than any other. Of course, this is with reference to their impact on the music world.

The Beatles, along with one or two others, are the bedrock of what we presently know as the Rock 'n Roll phenomenon. From the release of their single "I Want To Hold Your Hand" in 1963, to their dissolution in 1971, this group was on the cutting edge of all that makes up Rock. Paul McCartney, John Lennon, George Harrison, and Ringo Starr began in the dives of Liverpool and from there hit the world with "Beatlemania." The fascinating success

of the Beatles also triggered the "British invasion" —
the domination of the American charts by British
bands.

The music of the Beatles was head and shoulders
above almost all other Rock groups concerning
influence. The Beatles now have more than 60
million-selling records, and have sold well over 400
million worldwide. They were some of the first
musicians to use the technique of "backward
masking." The single-most influential album in the
history of Rock was the 1967 "Sergeant Peppers
Lonely Hearts Club Band." This recording changed
the complexion of Rock to a much more
introspective, message-oriented vehicle. The
awesome success of the Beatles should not surprise
the informed Christian, the reason being that they
were completely anti-Christ.

The press officer of the Beatles, Derek Taylor, was
quoted as saying that the group was much more anti-
Christ than he was, and he was very much so. He
further said that the "boys" often shocked him which
was not a simple thing to do.

Paul McCartney once said in an interview with
Playboy Magazine that none of the group had any
belief in God. John Lennon, a self-proclaimed non-
believer, made the now-infamous statement,
"Christianity will go, we're more popular than Jesus
now." George Harrison was a very avid follower of
the Maharishi Mahesh Yogi. Harrison was a
practicing Hindu in the late '60's.

The Beatles wrote and recorded far too many
songs to mention in our limited space; however, some

of the drug-related tunes include "Hey Jude," "Fixing a Hole," and "Lucy in the Sky with Diamonds." Subliminals include "Revolution 9" and "I AM a Walrus." One song secretly advocates the use of pot, and the other was probably used for the hype that told the world that Paul was dead. This was done in order to become even more powerful.

After having all that the world had to offer, Paul McCartney was arrested recently in Japan for drug possession. Ringo Starr is seldom seen without the pentagram around his neck. George Harrison has sunk deeper and deeper into his obsession with spiritualism. And John Lennon was murdered in New York in December of 1980.

BLACK SABBATH   (SE, D, R, FR, SA)

Black Sabbath is undoubtedly one of the blackest groups ever to come upon the Rock scene. The band was formed in late 1969 in the United Kingdom and was first named "Earth." However, because of their occult involvement and practices, they changed to Black Sabbath and arrived upon a plan of national acclaim.

They hit the charts with very little publicity and a certain amount of critical scorn. Theirs was very much an "underground" breakthrough, bypassing the usual media channels. This should let anyone know that Satan can do anything that pleases him in the making of successful bands.

Ozzy Osbourne was the lead singer for Black Sabbath until recently. This young man is one of the most bizarre of all Rock musicians. He seems totally possessed by the powers of darkness.

Black Sabbath defined the type of Rock that is now known as "heavy metal." (Explained in glossary of terms) In 1970 they recorded an album entitled "Paranoid," and immediately categorized themselves as a "black magic show" powered by loud music. On the cover of the album "We Sold Our Soul to Rock 'N Roll" all of the "S's" are Satanic S's. Their latest album cover is beyond description. The album is named "The Mob Rules," and has a grotesque picture of a torture rack with witches holding whips. The rack is empty, but blood is splattered over it, the wall behind, and the stones on the ground. A cross hangs on the rack which is symbolic of the crucifixion. There is a piece of cloth on the rack which is representative of the "shroud of Christ." The rack is wired like an electric chair and rigged like a gas chamber. This cover was one of the most horrible I observed in my research.

Bill Ward, the group's drummer, said in an interview with *Rolling Stone* that Satan was probably God. Geezer Butler, bassist, said that he could see the devil whenever he played. In fact, he went so far as to say that *he was* Lucifer.

Beware of this group! Whenever you see anything connected with Black Sabbath — get rid of it!!

BLACK OAK ARKANSAS (SE, R, SA)

Black Oak Arkansas was once just a place. It would certainly have been better if it had remained only that. This group has very little to say for itself except for filthy album covers and raunchy sex lyrics.

The band first came together in 1965. They were previously named "Knowbody Else." They were former school rebels led by singer Jim Dandy. Black Oak toured Great Britain in 1974 with Black Sabbath and afterward became a high-grossing box office attraction themselves.

In 1973 the group recorded the album "Raunch and Roll," which uses the technique of backward masking in the song, "When Electricity Came to Arkansas." They say, "Satan, Satan, Satan, he is god, he is god, he is god." This statement is immediately followed by a demonic laugh. There is also the chanting of prayers which are used in Satan worship. Please do not be so curious as to listen to this without the protection of the blood of Christ.

The group owns tracts of land around Black Oak, Arkansas, and lives there.

BLONDIE   (SE, D, R)

Blondie is the name of the group, not the girl singer. This group is the first to break out of the "Punk" or "New Wave" scene and become reasonably successful in Rock. Deborah Harry is the explanation for the seeming breakthrough. She is a vampish ex-Playboy bunny with punchy vocals and an overpowering stage presence. Blondie is a New York band that came to national prominence in 1979 with a hit single, "Heart of Glass." Deborah Harry emerged as the press-acclaimed sex symbol of the cynical '70's.

Harry is reported as saying that she always felt that she was a woman with a man's brain...a man locked in a woman's body.

Some of the songs recorded by Blondie are "In the Flesh," "Rapture," and "Rip Her to Shreds." The latest album was reviewed by *Rolling Stone* as TERRIBLE. However, they said it was so bad that it was perversely fascinating.

Deborah performs practically nude; hence, the reason for the large crowds.

BLUE OYSTER CULT (SE, D, R, FR, SA)

Blue Oyster Cult is one of the heaviest of the "heavy metal" groups. The Cult is extremely demonic and performs with enough decibels to shake the fillings out of its fans' teeth.

The group started in 1971 in New York. Its philosophy is mirrored in its logo — a Satanic cross.

BOC's first national album was "Tyranny and Mutation." "Agents of Fortune" has a picture of a man holding tarot cards with a message saying, "He who comes against the power faces death." The album "Cultosarus Erectus" shows a large creature with a small spacecraft displaying the Satanic cross. "Some Enchanted Evening" has a picture of a black horse with a Satanic cross on the bridle. "Fire of Unknown Origins" shows witches with empty eyes displaying pentagrams and Santanic crosses.

"Spectres" has a picture of the group in a seance calling up the dead, or a demon. The song, "The Reaper," relates the story of a suicide pact as a way to show your ultimate love.

It does not take a very discerning Christian to be aware the Blue Oyster Cult is a messenger of the adversary in an overtly direct manner.

I still like my oysters on the half shell.

MARC BOLIN AND T REX   (D, SA)

Bolin began to perform in 1966. From his early days, he was totally engrossed with the occult, mythologies, and prophecy. He steadily progressed in the success syndrome until 1972, when through the album "Slider," Bolin became a teen idol.

He and his band, T Rex, an abbreviatd name for Tyrannosaurus Rex, were English. They exported their message to the American youth through albums like "Prophets, Seers, and Sages." The driving message of Bolin and T Rex was wizards, witches, demons, and last-minute salvation by the means of Rock 'n Roll.

One album cover depicts the spiritual world with people in hell carrying heavy boulders being guarded by demons and a woman on a horse. The title of this album is "My People Were Fair and Had Sky in Their Hair...But Now They're Content to Wear Stars on Their Brows."

Marc Bolin was killed on September 16, 1977, in an automobile accident with Gloria Jones driving. Jones was the woman he left his wife and family to live with. As we have said, the devil can kill, and kill he does.

GRAHAM BOND (D, SA)

Bond was called by some "the father of British rhythm and blues." He had his biggest days of success in the late 1960's. Both Bond and his wife shared an interest in magic.

In 1974, after the simultaneous collapse of his band and his marriage, he drifted into a downward spiral. Over the years his drug addiction worsened, and he ultimately suffered a complete nervous breakdown. He died mysteriously under the wheels of a train in London at the the age of 37.

His friends reported that he was completely obsessed by worship in the occult. He believed he was Aleister Crowley's son. Crowley was the most popular spiritualist in England, and was so evil that he nicknamed himself "the beast - 666."

BOSTON (FR)

Boston was formed in 1976 and had a double-platinum album the same year. This is unprecedented. The group derived its name from its home.

Boston performs straight-ahead Rock 'n Roll. They were masterminded by Tom Scholz, a former designer for Polaroid. The logo of the group is a spacecraft. The cover of their album "Boston" pictures a spacecraft destroying earth. They have been so successful that the group left a very large check, which was their part of a concert, at a concert hall for over one year. $250,000 forgotten??

DAVID BOWIE (SE, D, R, FR)

David Bowie capitalized upon weirdness in order to break into a worldwide market. He performs in dresses and female makeup. His early trademark was orange hair and bizarre mannerisms.

Bowie was born in London. He changed his name from David Jones to David Bowie in order not to clash with the already known David Jones of Monkee fame. Bowie is obsessed with the collapse of civilization and science fiction. With the sci-fi theme, he claims to be able to see the future as evidenced by his double album "Stage" and 1980 release "Scary Monsters."

The album cover of "Chameleon" pictures Bowie in the forms of both man and woman. On "Scary Monsters" Bowie is seen dressed as a woman. Bowie is a leader of the homosexual/bisexual movement in the world of Rock.

BUFFALO SPRINGFIELD (D, R)

The Buffalo Springfield was *the* group of the 1960's. It was formed on the west coast in 1966 by Stephen Stills and Neil Young. Young and Stills frequently feuded and, subsequently, the Springfield broke up. Young was extremely enigmatic and unpredictable. To this day he retains a Messianic following. The Springfield was an advocate of the pulling down of society through revolution. However, the members could not stop fighting long enought to actualize their philosophy. Down and out in the third round.

CANNED HEAT   (D)

Canned Heat was formed in 1966 in California and became very popular after the 1967 Monterrey Music Festival. They were basically a blues band with a flair for Rock.

The band fell upon numerous tragedies in the few short years of its peak. Members quit and rejoined too often to mention for fear of confusion. Bob "the Bear" Hite and Alan "Blind Owl" Wilson were the driving forces behind the group. Hite was a grocery store sack boy, and Wilson was a music major from Boston University. Wilson was considered one of the foremost authorities on "blues" at the time of his death.

Wilson died of a drug overdose on September 3, 1970, in the backyard of Bob Hite. Hite died in April of 1981 of an apparent heart attack. However, it is reported that his death was also drug related. After the death of Wilson, Canned Heat's work was significantly inferior.

The heat is finally off.

CHEAP TRICK   (SE, R, D)

This group is a late runner in the fad music called "New Wave." It has been reviewed as clumsy, unimaginative, repetitive, and derivative. Its members are deviates of the highest order.

The group was formed in Illinois in 1977 and tried the narrow ground between put-on and pretense. It is powered by strong and loud Rock 'n Roll.

The members of Cheap Trick display the attributes of maniacs with extremely weird antics. For example, on the album cover of "Dream Police" everyone is dressed in white as if to portray a dream. A female mannequin hangs partially dismembered while one of the members holds the chain saw that was used to cut her up. Sick, huh? What a cheap trick!

CLASH   (SE, R, D)

The Clash is one of the more hyped of the English "New Wave" bands. It was formed in early 1976 in the working class pubs of London. Like most of the "Punk" groups, their music is aggressive and primitive. On stage they are a complete audio-visual experience. They advocate sex, drugs, violence, and rebellion. Their 1975 tour was named "Anarchy."

The album "London's Calling" portrays the group destroying their instruments. On the cover of "Black Market Clash" the group is seen inciting a riot. The album "Sandinista" was reviewed like this, ."..the Clash have lost their bearings and find themselves going round and round in a cul-de-sac." However, they are popular because they simply project the howl of teenage anger from the concrete jungle neighborhoods of London.

ALICE COOPER   (SE, R, D, RF, SA)

Alice Cooper was born Vincent Furnier on February 4, 1948. He is the son of a protestant minister. This is usually the first thing that the press picks up. He formed his hype-powered approach in 1968 after linking up with manager Shep Gordon. Alice is Rock 'n Roll weirdness at its zenith. His antics are seldom topped. He mimics making love on stage with a six-foot boa constrictor. He also makes love to a corpse. The song "Cold Ethyl" speaks of necrophilia (having sex with the dead). The stage show madness goes so far as to act out sado/masochistic fantasies. Alice chops up life-like babies and throws blood capsules over the stage and audience. He supposedly got the name Alice Cooper from an experience with a ouija board in which he was guaranteed worldwide fame if he would change his name to that of the witch Alice Cooper. Since this time, Cooper claims to be the reincarnated witch of the 17th century.

Alice says that the basis of his group is rebellion. He claims that kids look up to him because he belittles their parents. He participates regularly in seances and other forms of witchcraft.

While claiming to be normal by having hobbies

such as golf and fishing, Alice Cooper remains one of the most dangerous of all of the Rock musicians.

The album cover of "Special Forces" shows Cooper wearing Satanic medals. The album "Muscle of Love" (self-explanatory) is covered in brown paper as if it were pornography in the mail. My wife once rode a plane with Cooper and his stage band. She said. "STRANGGGGEEEEE!"

ELVIS COSTELLO (D, SE)

Elvis Costello was born in England and hit upon the popularity scene in 1977 when he released a demonic ballad about a girl totally engrossed in a television cop show. He has hit the top of the charts as a performer and a songwriter. His songs are categorized as the toughest and most alienated music of the day. This young man is extremely ruthless and distant. He projects deep bitterness and is at times hostile to both fans and press alike. He writes about sex as if God didn't have anything to do with it. He is reviewed as a very unique musical talent, but a completely unsatisfying performer. Elvis who?

CRAZY HORSE (D, SE)

This west coast group was formed to be backup for Neil Young. Its philosophy was sex and drugs. The group disbanded in 1972 after the drug-related death of Danny Whitten, but was revived in 1975 by Young to dedicate an album to their comrad who had OD'd. The title of the album was "Tonight's the

Night" and it introduced the song "The Needle and the Damage Done."

Crazy Horse projected hard acid Rock with a message from hell.

CREEDENCE CLEARWATER REVIVAL (D)

Every member of CCR was born in the San Francisco Bay area and went to high school together. They formed a band called the Blue Velvets in 1964. After signing a contract with a record company in early '65, their name was changed to the Golliwogs.

Before having one of the largest series of hit singles of any group in the '60's and '70's, they cut a whole string of flops. However, in a make-or-break effort, they changed their name to *Creedence Clearwater Revival* and literally exploded on the music scene to become the most popular '50's-oriented white Rock 'n Roll band in existence.

CCR was powered by the raspy voice and songwriting genius of John Fogerty. Fogerty wrote songs about drugs, the south, and sex...not necessarily in that order. The CCR couldn't stand the pressure, greed, and phenomenal success. They broke up in 1972. They are beyond revival now! I know some people like that...!

THE DAMNED (SE, D, R)

The Damned was formed in the summer of 1975. They were forerunners in the English New Wave movement.

Musically the group follows the manic stage antics of the Punk Rock scene. They play forcefully loud with an emphasis on sex, drugs, and violence. The "Punk Rock" world has its base in rebellion. The clothes, haircuts, and lifestyles in general project the bottom of the degradation barrel.

The Damned are truly damned...and damning others along the way.

DEEP PURPLE   (SE, D, R, SA)

Deep Purple, a British band, had its mystical beginnings in Germany during the winter of 1968. The group had roots in the occult from its inception, but later became identified with ear-drum bursting "heavy metal" Rock.

The personnel changed almost daily because of friction and illness. At the outset of "heavy metal" music, the Purple was recorded as playing at such high decibel levels that 24 actual cases of up to 90% deafness for over 36 hours was documented by the opponents of hard Rock following a live performance of the band.

Deep Purple albums are considered classics by avid Rock fans. Spin-off players from Deep Purple have joined such groups as Nazareth and other occultish performers.

Tommy Bolin, an American, was brought into the band in 1975. He died of a drug overdose in Miami in December of 1976. The death of Bolin marked the beginning of the end for Deep Purple. They disbanded in 1976.

Richie Blackmoore, now with Rainbow, is a leading proponent of the occult.

THE DEAD BOYS   (SE, D, R)

The Dead Boys are a "Punk Rock" group formed in Cleveland, Ohio. They received their first taste of success on the New York "Punk" scene in 1976.

Their message is the same as other New Wave groups...namely rebellion, sex, drugs, and violence. They play loud, unintelligible Rock with stage antics that portray the mentally deranged. They appear decidedly weired while performing their songs, "Young, Loud and Snotty" and "We Have Come for Your Children."

Most "Punk" group members change their names to that which fits their philosophy; such as Rat Scabies, Sid Vicious, Johnny Rotten, Jimmy Zero, Jeff Magnum, and Stiv Bators. There are other names which define where these deranged young people are "coming from."

Stiv Bators of the Dead Boys said, "If I'm too loud for you, then you're too old for me...I want your children."

In some areas of the country...on selected airways...in white-line fever drug clubs...they are succeeding. Our children are definitely being affected.

DEVO   (SE, D)

The name Devo is short for de-evolution. It implies an already-completed state of dementia. Dementia is defined as loss of mental powers. Consequently, the Akron, Ohio, group projects a message of automation. In this Rock 'n Roll vehicle, the future is depicted as being mechanical and computer oriented...devoid of personality and emotion. People are simply automations.

Devo has recorded songs such as "Whip It" and "Be Stiff" (songs about masturbation). These recordings have very pointed lyrics which are more than just sexually suggestive.

The group is usually seen in aluminum jump suits as they perform their synthesizer-oriented music.

On the album cover of "Freedom of Choice" the group is pictured making a mockery of human volition. The album cover of "Duty Now for the Future" pictures Devo with no faces...names stamped upon their foreheads, and the "all-powerful" computer working in the backgound.

DR. HOOK   (SE, D, R)

Dr. Hook was formerly Dr. Hook and the Medicine Show. The band was formed in 1972 as a novelty act for Playboy cartoonist and songwriter Shel Silverstien. The group is American, and has run the total gamut of musical styles. They have been successful performing Rock, country, and disco. Even now, they defy a particular label. Their stage show antics border on the bizarre. They sing about sex, drugs, and economy. They were bankrupt at one time, but have been tenacious enough to regroup and continue worldwide tours. Founder-member George Cumings left the group in 1975 after suffering a complete nervous collapse.

The album cover of "Pleasure and Pain" pictures a tear from one mask and saliva from the other mask. "Pleasure and Pain" signifies sado/masochistic fantasies.

This group is seen in commercials for big name commodities...if the producers only knew!

THE DOOBIE BROTHERS   (SE, D)

The Doobies were originally a hard Rock trio called Pud. They were formed in California during the year of 1969 by ex-Mody Grape, ex-Jefferson Airplane drumer Skip Spence. Several musicians were sitting around smoking a joint...a doobie. They decided on a name —The Doobie Brothers. The group signed a Warner Brothers contract in 1971, added three more pieces and became the Doobies, a la the Allman Brothers.

The Doobies are exemplary of the '70's music, recording a variety of hard and soft Rock. They have the same philosophy as many of the Rock bands of that era as they project songs like "Living on the Fault Line." On the album cover of "What Were Once Vices are Now Habits," the band is seen in hell with thousands of fans.

I have just heard that The Doobies have embarked on their farewell tour. They are breaking up!

THE DOORS   (SE, D, R, FR)

The Doors was formed in 1965 by Jim Morrison and Ray Manzarek. Both were students at UCLA at the time. The remainder of the band was found in a meditation center and were playing under the name of Psychedelic Rangers.

The Doors had its beginning through the support of the underground, but by the time of the release of its first album, became one of the leading Rock groups in the United States.

Jim Morrison was nothing short of crazy. His songs established him as having one of the most bizarre minds of his time. Morrison was totally preoccupied with sex and death. Drugs were so common in what he advocated that the trend of the '60's was actually centered around his philosophy.

The "Rock Star" phenomenon completely engrossed Morrison. It is said that he lived on a continuous stage. His personality was volital and his friendships few.

The album "Waiting for the Sun" contained an inside sleeve with a full libretto of "The Celebration of the Lizard King." "Lizard King" was a name that was subsequently given to Morrison. The sleeve was a narrative poem based on the beliefs of the Shaman and other Oriental philosophies.

Morrison had several skirmishes with the law. In 1967 he was rousted by a policeman for having sex with a young girl in the open area backstage of a concert hall. During the night's show, he went into tirade about the incident to such a degree that the police turned on the house lights and arrested him on stage. A riot immediately ensued.

Morrison was also arrested outside a topless go-go club in Las Vegas after starting a fight with a security guard.

In March of 1969 Morrison was charged with lewd and lascivious behavior, indecent exposure, open profanity and public drunkenness. He was found guilty after a long trial.

Morrison was also arrested for drunkenness aboard an aircraft, and drunkenness after falling asleep on an old woman's porch in Los Angeles.

He became disillusioned and quit the band to take a rest in Paris. For years he had overindulged his body with drugs an alcohol. On July 3, 1971, he died of a drug-related heart attack in his bath. His widow died of an overdose of heroin in May of 1974.

Jim Morrison was an incorrigible rebel, totally committed to a course of self-destruction. He studied Nietzsche and William Blake, from which he derived the name of "The Doors."

The three Doors that remained carried on for a short time, but soon went their separate ways, thus ending one of the more devastating bands and personalities in the history of the demonical Rock scene.

EAGLES   (SE, D, SA)

The Eagles were organized in 1971 out of the wreckage of Linda Ronstadt's backup band. They are a California-based group. During the period of 1972 to 1976, they graduated into the most successful country-Rock group in the nation. Having built a steady cult following, the Eagles broke into the British scene in 1975 with the album "One of These Nights." According to *Time* magazine in a 1975 article, the Eagles got their name from the major spirit in the India cosmos. Many of their songs, as laid back as they may seem, derive their lyrics from the occultish writings of Carlos Castaneda. The group supposedly has an ongoing relationship with Anton Lavey, high priest of the United Church of Satan. The album "Hotel California" has a picture of a man who is probably Mr. Lavey on the album sleeve.

The songs, "Witchy Woman," "Good Day in Hell," "Journey of a Sorcerer," and others would let one know that the Eagles have roots in the prince of darkness. "Life in the Fast Lane" is an expression of the total despair and utter folly of the Rock music scene.

Writing music under the influence of the Indian drug Payote is a steady practice for this "middle-of-the-road" band.

The Eagles are established as the major hit-makers of single songs for a two-year period in the latter '70's. The youth of the world have made them rich. They have since disbanded.

ELECTRIC LIGHT ORCHESTRA   (D, FR, SA)

The ELO was originally launched in 1971 as a part of member Roy Wood's preoccupation with orchestral Rock, a la the Beatles. Wood dropped out early and left the ELO to more electric leanings. It is said that ELO resembles a symphony orchestra being made to play Rock 'n Roll at gun point.

When Wood left the ELO I, he left to form a band called Wizzard. ELO II was formed in 1973 and assembled the strangest types of musicians on the scene at that time. The reviews were largely indifferent; however, the primary reason for keeping the group alive was the original commitment to take up where the Beatles left off.

ELO is a British band, and uses the technique of "backward masking." On the album "Face the Music," before the song, "Fire is High," backward masking is used to explain that music is reversible, but time is not...turn back time...turn back time. The music of this song is used as the theme song for "Wide World of Sports."

The album cover "Eldorado" pictures a witch grabbing a red shoe which appears magical. The cover of "Face the Music" pictures an electric chair with stereo earphones for the head. True enough! Sit down and fry, kids!

EMERSON LAKE AND PALMER   (SE, D, R)

Emerson, Lake and Palmer are considered the architects of British "techno Rock." They perform with approximately thirty tons of equipment including highly sophisticated computers. It is said that they are the "Rock off-spring" of computer science.

The group was formed in 1969 after an aborted attempt to link up with Jimi Hendrix. Each member was already seasoned in the music world, coming from groups such as The Nice, King Crimson, and Atomic Rooster.

Emerson had established a reputation for daring acrobatics such as knife throwing, instrument destruction and general musical sadism. The group became a furiously-active stage show with such antics as keyboard burning, dagger throwing, hydraulic elevation of instruments, and bizarre stunts which created a very expensive performance. However, as you know by now, the crowds went wild. The fans actually paid for the destructive inclinations of the group.

Emerson, while with The Nice, was banned from a concert hall in London after burning the American flag in an earlier performance. ELP performs at such a decibel level that deafness is the result for many of the fans immediately following a concert. At one time they toured with a 64-piece orchestra, and during the grand finale Emerson's keyboard would burst into flames. ELP's lyrics depict the band's philosophy as sex, violence, drugs, and more prevalently, rebellion.

FLEETWOOD MAC   (SE, D, R, FR, SA)

Fleetwood Mac derives its name from the last names of the group's drummer, Mick Fleetwood, and bassist, John McVie. The band was originally launched in England in 1967 and appeared as a hard core blues act.

Fleetwood Mac soon developed a large following and stuck to proven British blues formulas. However, as they evolved, they began to experiment more and more. In 1969, the band suffered a major shake-up through a drastic change in personnel. Founder, Peter Green retired and Jeremy Spencer joined the religious cult, "The Children of God." After this, the group began to drift from their original style to more mellow sounds.

In the early '70's, the former manager put another group on the road with the same name. Furious court battles took place and the original were victorious, only to soon lose another driving force in the person of Bob Welch.

"Mac" regrouped, operating from a Los Angeles base with husband and wife team Lindsey Buckingham and Stevie Nicks (a self-professed witch).

The album art for many of Fleetwood Mac's discs are filled with Satanic subtleties. On the album, "Rumors," there is a man with a crystal ball depicting fortune-telling. The song "Rhiannon," written by Stevie Nicks, is about a witch in Wales. The lyrics for the group are published by the Welsh Witch Publishing Co.

Frequently, in their concerts, Stevie Nicks steps to the front of the stage and dedicates the night to all of the witches of the world. She is currently making a movie in which she plays the witch Rhiannon.

Fleetwood Mac is the core of a COVEN. The members study witchcraft and practice magic.

Quite obviously, one of the reasons for the fact that the group is extremely popular on the airways is their allegience to Satan... THE god OF ROCK.

FOGHAT   (SE, D, R)

This group is a carbon copy of another English band, Savoy Brown. They, too, are British and still remain relatively obscure in their own country, yet highly popular in the States. This is due to their concert appeal. They play hard-driving blues boogie at a decibel level that is internally destructive to the uninitiated.

If one were to see a young person wearing a Foghat tee-shirt, he could rest assured that the youth's musical tastes have found the "scrapings of the pan."

Drugs, sex, and rebellion are the messages projected by these musicians who rely upon guitars, extended solos, long songs, and loud volume to exist.

There are so many of you guys... who knows the difference?

FOREIGNER   (SE, D, R)

This band is another English phenomenon. It appeared in 1977 after being formed from the leftovers of several other already-established groups. Their hit single "Feels Like the First Time" came from their debut album bearing the name of the group.

The music is standard British formula with mind-rending volume and speed rhythm-and-blues riffs. Wailing vocals and the normal appearances of the band lets one know at a glance that this group has been cloned by the manipulators of the stadium Rock.

The album cover of the disc "Head Games" has a teenage girl sitting on a male urinal in a men's room writing on the wall. This grotesque picture is a take-off on the term "head." It also has bisexual advocations. The standard three...sex, drugs and rebellion are the projected messages of Foreigner.

PETER FRAMPTON (SE)

Peter Frampton remains an enigma to most critics of the Rock music scene. He was born in April of 1950 in Kent, England. Frampton is a CLASSIC example of easy come, easy go. He came out of nowhere in 1976 with his first album "Frampton Comes Alive" which immediately went gold, and then platinum. He was catipulted to the scale of international superstar almost overnight. He had been around for a short time with groups like the Herd and Humble Pie and was always picked out from the other members as the pin-up boy of the British bopper press.

His highly-successful album generated 50 million dollars of income in one year's time. It became one of the top ten best-selling albums of *all* time.

Frampton sang about what he was projected to be... A MAJOR SEX SYMBOL. The lyrics of songs such as "I'm in YOU," "Baby, I Love Your Way," "Do You Feel," are more than suggestive. They are explicit!

Many were at a loss to explain the sudden success of this baby-faced guitar player. That success came to an end in 1979 when, according to his own admission, Frampton could not handle the sudden rise to stardom. He turned to drugs and alcohol to cope.

In 1980 a major Frampton concert was cancelled due to lack of advance ticket sales. The general response was, "Peter who?"

This prince of the airways ceases to empower that which becomes "has-been" or unmarketable to the buying public. As we say...here today, gone tomorrow!

GRAND FUNK RAILROAD (SE, D, R, SA)

Grand Funk was the first Rock band to be declared totally and irrevocably "HYPE." Mark Farner, Mel Schacher, Don Brewer, and Craig Frost comprised the first train to "boot hill."

The Funk surfaced in Flint, Michigan, during the late 1960's. They were reviled and loathed by Rock critics of the day. Ironically, however, while they were highly ridiculed by the establishment, they were one of the most popular bands in the country. Anything anti-establishment was making it back then.

They had a string of hit singles and albums and a list of sold out concerts a mile long. Their music? Loud, heavy metal, and bombastic in explosion. Rod Stewart once said of them, "Grand Funk is the all-time loud white noise."

Terry Knight, a Detroit disc jockey, saw "gold" and became the spokesman for the group. He landed them a slot at the 1969 Atlanta Pop Festival, and the rest is history. The crowd went bonkers and the record companies began to call.

Grand Funk knocked out six straight gold albums and sold out New York's Shea Stadium — not once, but twice.

Capitol Records enshrined Grand Funk Railroad high above Times Square during the costly promotion of their album "Closer to Home" in 1970. At that time, the billboard cost approximately $33,500 for the paint job, and $7,000 a month for the space.

Knight promoted the band to the height of "heavy metal" fame in this country, but Britain held the group at arm's length probably because of its own superior groups of the same sort.

The group never regained its momentum after a vicious court controversy in which Knight had sued for control of the Railroad and was defeated. It was downhill from that point, and in 1976, before the group's album "Born to Die," there was an unpublicized decision to split up.

The Funks were never accepted for their artistic ability; consequently, the more they tried, the less records they sold. Finally, the train stopped...*at* "boot hill."

The album "All the Girls of the World Beware" was produced by the band in order to introduce the "spirit" influences of the dark world of "heavy metal." During the years of the late '60's and throughout the middle '70's, Grand Funk Railroad was churning out songs advocating illicit sex of all forms, drugs, rebellion, and inferences dealing with the "spirit world."

They will remain the earliest and foremost exponents of tuneless, metallic, thrashing, heavyweight noise this country has ever produced. Old trains never die...they just become enshrined.

THE GRATEFUL DEAD   (SE, D, R, FR, SA)

Reported to be the greatest San Francisco band of all time, The Grateful Dead have survived not only the waning of the "electric '60's," but the '70's as well. Their faithful legends of "dead-heads" are still intact.

This group grew out of the hodge-podge of Frisco's early musical conglomeration of country, Rock folk, and blues, all fueled by LSD. They were a product of the hippie drug culture.

The Dead was formed in 1959 with Jerry Garcia and others of the immediate pre-Dead group called the Warlocks. As the '60's dragged on, the band came to know Ken Kesey's Merry Pranksters and their "chemical enlightment." It was under the influence of LSD and other drugs that the Warlocks became The Grateful Dead.

This was the documented period of "the Acid Tests of 1965." Acid was legal in California until 1966, and during the time preceding its banning, The Grateful Dead performed their colorful musical tapestries to all of the freaks who were experimenting. Thus, they became immediate heros of San Francisco's burgeoning underground. This was the illicit background for the group.

The band's name, the Grateful Dead, comes from a collection of folk ballads by Francis Child. Next to the Jefferson Airplane, The Death epitomizes the flower-power era. Jerry Garcia once said that acid Rock music was simply what a person listened to when he was high on acid.

The group is reported to have one of the largest sound systems in the world. Their concerts are characterized by the second-generation hippie who seemingly cannot grow up.

They have had the similar hassles of other groups that have been together for awhile — such as court proceedings against managers, drug charges against the members, etc. There have been at least two busts during the performances of The Dead that have resulted in prison sentences for several of them. Ron "Pig-Pen" McKernan died in 1973 from an accumulation of drugs and alcohol.

Their album art projects death by way of their logo which is a skull or skeleton. Their songs advocate drugs, sex, rebellion, false religions, Satan and other messages of the "age of revolution" in this country.

I have been where The Grateful Dead came from, and to be sure ... it is a sad sight indeed. Jerry Garcia admits that the lives of the members of the group are controlled by music. In recent years the band has mellowed ... yet they still turn out the message of the underworld.

THE GUESS WHO (SE, D, R)

The Guess Who was formed in 1960 by Burton Cummings and Randy Bachman. It became Canada's top singles band originating in the Winnipeg area.

The group reached a level of success by having its own local television show. Cummings adopted the singing mannerisms of Jim Morrison, and Bachman caught center stage through derivative, but effective, guitar riffs.

The Guess Who crashed onto the singles scene with the hit "These Eyes." This led to a string of million sellers.

In 1971 Bachman, sick and in need of rest from touring, quit the group. Bachman, a converted Morman, could not stomach the band's on-tour lifestyle. Without Bachman, the group trudged on, dipping into social criticism, hoping for the illusive market of the "hip" movement. Bachman went on to form Bachman Turner Overdrive, which was to become Canada's number one band.

In 1975 after numerous personnel changes, The Guess Who decided to call it quits. They ended industry speculation by announcing the formal dissolution. At the height of their popularity in 1970, record sales for The Guess Who grossed an estimated 5 million dollars.

When one says, "Guess who," one usually hears, "I don't know — who?" No one seems to remember life's important things! Oh, well!

JIMI HENDRIX (SE, D, R, FR, SA)

Jimi Hendrix has become a legend in the world of rock music. It has been a haunting legend, but on the other hand, a very influential one. Hendrix was born November 27, 1942, in Seattle, Washington. He remains Rock's most dynamic guitarist, even though he died of an overdose of drugs in 1970.

The early life of Jimi Hendrix was spent listening and playing along with blues guitar players such as Muddy Waters, B.B. King, and Robert Johnson. Hendrix managed to expand the horizons of the Rock music scene by taking the blues into the psychedelic and even harder Rock veins without losing sight of the roots.

He began his illustrious career after being discharged from the military in 1963 for medical reasons. No one knows what specifically. Hendrix went on the road with already established artists such as Wilson Pickett, Jackie Wilson and Little Richard. He then went to Greenwich Village to make it on his own and was discovered by Chas Chandler. Chandler, recognizing Hendrix's potential, took him back to London where the Jimi Hendrix Experience was formed.

The group became an immediate success. The impact was "barn-storming" and amazing. After two hit singles, a record contract was formed with Track Records.

The Experience performed very powerful psychedelic blues, which was the heaviest Rock heard at the time. Hendrix himself appeared very cool and seemed to stir the sexual fantasies of white females. It is significant to note that his audiences were virtually entirely white.

The Jimi Hendrix Experience came to America in 1967 to perform at the Monterrey Pop Festival, which also launched Janis Joplin and Otis Redding. It was an event arranged by Beatle Paul McCartney. The performance was recorded on film and remains in extreme demand even now.

Hendrix soon cut three enormously successful albums — one of which featured nude women on the cover. This was to overtly capitalize on his "sexual superstar" imagery. Most of the women on this particular cover are white. Hendrix came under pressure to form an all-black band in order to satisfy more hungry fantasies of the white audience. He did this in 1969 with a group called Band of Gypsies.

In August of 1969 he appeared at Woodstock and performed a version of the "Star Spangled Banner" that made him the hero of the massive movement of worldwide revolution. However, in August of 1970 he played a very strange and reportedly messy set at the Isle of Wright, and in September of the same year Hendrix died in London. The official cause of his death was inhalation of vomit following barbituate intoxication.

Jimi Hendrix had been the most important instrumentalist in the history of Rock. *Rolling Stone* said of him, "Hendrix was the first black performer to take on white Rock 'n Roll head-on and win."

Hendrix remains a symbol of the "psychedelic acid age." His music was bombastic and metallic. His lyrics were messages of illicit sex, "do-your-own-thing" in drugs, "let's overthrow all forms of authority," "all religions are acceptable," and "worship the god of the world...Satan." Superstar problems built up and surrounded him. He began to actually think he was God.

The song "Purple Haze" was listed in the psychedelic top 40 of all time, as was "Room Full of Mirrors." Hexdrix once said that music was a spirit in and of itself. People could be hypnotized with music and anything could be placed into their minds.

Although numerous albums have come on the scene since his death, Hendrix only approved of six prior to his overdose. On the album "Jimi Hendrix" eastern religion symbols are covering the cover.

Jimi Hendrix spent only four years in the spotlight, but he extended the message of Rock beyond imagination. His influence defies description. It is almost as if he made a deal with the devil himself. One wonders!

HAWKWIND (SE, D, FR)

Hawkwind was launched in the late 1960's in London. In the beginnings it was a very loose "perform anywhere for anything" kind of group. Their antics gained them a freak following in the Notting Hill area of London, and from there they became England's most popular psychedelic band.

Of course, a couple of drug busts helped to cement their followers who were attached to the philosophy and lifestyle of the members of the group. They were hailed as "the people's band," and "the last of the true underground bands."

The group's members immersed themselves in science fiction, keying on more spacey aspects of the last decade's music. Their specialty is the Space Ritual Road Show, complete with psychedelic lighting, piercing decibel level, and the worship of alien forces.

On the cover of the album recorded live in Liverpool Stadium entitled "Space Ritual Live," there is a nude woman standing before two panthers. Her arms are outstretched to the gods (all sorts) as a bow encircles her with the all-seeing eye at the top. Her head is covered with snakes and astro signs...the group's message pictured.

From the rapid personnel changes of Hawkwind, Motorhead was formed. Their lastest album projects their ultimate desire...it is entitled "Masters of the Universe."

IGGY POP AND THE STOOGES

Iggy Pop was born James Osterburg in 1947 in Ann Arbor, Michigan. He adopted the name Iggy when he became the lead singer for a local Detroit band called the Prime Movers. After visions came to him, he went on his own with the worst concoction of dementia that was on the scene at the time. This was pure pre-punk punk.

Iggy would pull out of his ragbag of outrageous onstage gambits such things as...throwing up on stage, being beaten up, indulging in fellatio with members of the audience, and other depths of depravity which gained the Stooges unprecedented notoriety. This was three-chord, slobbering punk seven years ahead of it's time.

Because of obvious reasons, the band split up and Iggy, drug drenched, began to mow yards. Thanks to David Bowie, he gained a new start. However, Iggy became crazier and weirder by the year. He crashed again and wound up in a Los Angeles mental ward. Again, it was Bowie who brought him out and turned him loose on the public with the album, "The Idiot." Well named. Thanks again, David!

Iggy is the spiritual father of what is now the punk scene. The album, "Metallic K.O." was originally recorded on a cassette. One can actually hear the band being pelted with beer bottles (a Punk tradition).

Iggy Pop and the Stooges did their last gig in the late'70's; yet, Iggy's reputation remains intact as rock's wildest and most bizarre performer. It is more bizarre than KISS, or Alice Cooper, or Ted Nugent, or AC⚡DC, or the Plasmatics, or etc., etc. Wow!

IRON BUTTERFLY   (SE, D, R)

One of the first of the super-successful "heavy metal" groups, Iron Butterfly left ground in San Diego, California, in 1968. Their first album was entitled "Heavy." However, as is the case with most Rock bands, group friction caused the loss of several members immediately after their debut.

Carrying four pieces, the Butterfly cut the monster-selling album "In A-Gadda-Da-Vida." This album became the first album ever to achieve platinum status. "In A-Gadda-Da-Vida" stayed on the charts for two years and contained the longest single ever recorded at the time. It featured an extended drum solo in the middle of the song which was long enough for the members of the group to leave stage during the concert and take a break.

The giant album became a millstone around the neck of the band as there was seemingly nothing they could do for an encore. After a farewell American tour in 1971, the Iron Butterfly returned to its cocoon and dissolved. However, they recently announced a re-birth. Maybe it isn't so!

"In A-Gadda-Da-Vida" is listed as number 13 on the all-time psychedelic top 40. The Butterfly was a symbol of the revolutionary '60's with its base in the hippie drug culture. Their lyrics were expressive of the decade's "big three"...drugs, sex and rebellion.

Iron — heavy! Butterfly — light...love! This group projected their philosophy by their name. Heavy light...or light heavy...or heavy love...or —

IRON MAIDEN

This group is relatively obscure "heavy metal" *molten madness* band that has recently come out with an album named, "The Number of the Beast 666."

The promotion for this album which was seen in a recent Billboard magazine pictures the skeleton of a Rock musician looming largely over the fiery pit of hell. The Devil himself stands second in command under the authority of the musician. (They just don't know.) Darkness is in the background, lightning is flashing, and hell is seen as being filled with millions of people and demons. The artwork is unbeliveably gross, but pictures the possibilities very well.

The copy for the promotion reads like this: IRON MAIDEN FORGED IN THE FIRES OF HELL — THE NEW ALBUM FROM THE MASTERS OF MOLTEN METAL MADNESS — THE BEAST ON THE ROAD and other "cute" sayings.

Iron Maiden is now on a rival with Judas Priest, Van Halen, Black Sabbath, and other bands that serve their god very well.

THE JEFFERSON AIRPLANE/STARSHIP
(SE, D, R, FR, SA)

The Jefferson Airplane was San Francisco's first and best-remembered "flower power" band. The group was formed in 1965 by Marty Balin and Paul Kantner and became a rallying point for the Haight Ashbury freak community. Consequently, they were heralded as national standard-bearers of young America's new-found revolutionary/drug consciousness.

Although the Airplane was shaky at the start, it became the first "Frisco" band to become a legend and the first to gain a major record contract.

Steve Spence, the original drummer of the group, quit early to begin Moby Grape in 1966. This brought about several other major changes, and also gave opportunity for the band to acquire the vocal abilities of Grace Slick.

She brought with her from the repertoire of her old band "The Great Society" such drug-glorifying songs as "White Rabbit" and songs advocating revolution such as "Volunteers." This record contained their battle cry, "Tear down the walls, Mother F-----s!" "Plastic Fastastic Lover" was also one of the band's earlier cuts. The title explains the content.

Then came 1969 . . . a year in which the love-peace vibe met its downfall. Drug busts were proliferated, and hippie panaceas were "old hat." The band became more political and expressive of their philosophy of free love and drugs. The less political co-founder, Balin, split and by 1972 the Airplane was stalling. It was 1972 when the group cut their famous album in which Jesus Christ was reported to be having an affair with Mary Magdalene.

After one of their ardent tours, Grace Slick became pregnant by co-founder Paul Kantner. She was reported to say that marriage was only for those who had the energy to go to the courthouse and fill out papers ... she would rather sit around and smoke dope.

There was dissention galore and several personnel changes during the floundering years. Slick left to produce her much-maligned solo album "Manhole." This means exactly what it implies. However, after much dissatisfaction on the part of all of the founding members of the Airplane, in 1974 the Jefferson Airplane became the Jefferson Starship with its wayward members back in the fold. The new incarnation album was "Red Octopus." It was like the Second Coming for the '60's counter-culture flag wavers.

To give an example of the power of rock musicians, Grace Slick bared her breasts while performing at Gaelic Park in the Bronx. When she did, it was reported that a major portion of the female audience did likewise. There were approximately 10,000 young girls who went topless. Rock concert photographers were then called "nipple-snappers." The film business must have been good that day.

The Jefferson Airplane/Starship reflects the counter-culture of ROCK MUSIC very well. They sang, sing and live the messages of perverted sex, drugs, rebellion, eastern religions and mysticism, and have put on track the message of Satan himself. They have been support group for the "Stones" during Satanic worship in concerts. They believe that music is God and that concerts are church.

Although they have had their problems and have suffered major changes, they have survived the transition era.

They are still very popular messengers of THE god OF ROCK. Beware of the roots of this "hardline" Rock band.

ELTON JOHN   (SE, D, R)

Elton John was born Reginald Kenneth Dwight on March 25, 1947, in Middlesex, England. John is one of the few stars to be identifiably confined to the '70's. For a period in the middle '70's, he was the largest-selling entertainer in the world.

He began his show business career playing keyboard for a group called Bluesology. Ultimately, this group came to the attention of R & B hero, Long John Baldry, who subsequently recruited the group to back him in 1967. It was then that Reginald Dwight decided that a better name was in order, so he borrowed the first name from the band's saxophone player, Elton Dean. The last came from Long John himself. Hence, Elton John.

After the demise of Bluesology, Elton John found himself unemployed. He answered an ad for "New Talent" in a local magazine. When he showed up for the interview, it was obvious that he had never sung.

He could, however, write music, so the agency matched him with Bernie Taupin, a lyricist. The team would later become a legend in the music industry.

By 1970 John had released his first album and was a huge success in America. His biggest hits came in the mid-'70's, and his concerts were followed by legions. By the late '70's, John's work began to wane. This was partly due to exhaustion and partly because the style of musical tales began to change. John's music has taken a turn toward progression — a new direction. Nevertheless, it remains to be seen whether he can duplicate his phenomenal success of the '70's.

Elton John is an admitted bisexual. In an interview with the *Rolling Stone*, he conceded that he is both bisexual and suicidal. He said, "I crave to be loved, and I see nothing wrong with going to bed with somebody of your own sex. I think people should draw the line only at goats."

On the album cover of "The Yellow Brick Road," John is pictured stepping into the "gay" world. This album is said to be his finest. On the cover of "Captain Fantastic and the Brown Dirt Cowboy," John is pictured sitting on top of a piano which is the lid for hell. Demons and other depictions observe a man in a glass bowl with a watch (denoting time) on his back. The song "Levon" is anti-Christ. Jesus is portrayed as a cartoon balloon blower. The popularity of this bisexual is truly incredible. His annual income is reported at 7 million dollars. He is said to have taken out a 25 million dollar insurance policy on his life.

His tastes are extravagant and his lifestyle lascivious...yet he remains one of the most celebrated musicians of our time, being on display in Madame Tussaud's wax museum. When time is finished, and our Lord returns with the awesome power of judgment, where will people turn...to Elton John, the bisexual?

JOURNEY (SE, D)

Journey was formed in late 1973 by former members of the cultish band Santana. They made their debut in San Francisco on New Year's eve, and their second gig was before a crowd of 100,000 at Diamond Head Crater in Hawaii. This group has emerged as one of the five top straight-forward Rock concert bands in the current "stadium Rock phenomenon."

Journey has fought an identity crisis from the beginning. It is difficult for the layman to tell the difference between them and several other groups of the same trend. However, Journey fans are smart and loyal. Numerous changes in the line-up have given them an edge and a niche for the purposes of identification. Wherever the group winds up musically, one can be sure that their fans will be there with them.

Journey portrays emerging space crafts on their albums. Steve Perry, vocalist, says, "They say hard Rock can't have class, but we educate our audience to the degree of class that we feel they need to still have a good time." Journey is educating sell-out audiences from coast to coast without the support of the press or advertising. Whose support is behind this group? Guess!

JUDAS PRIEST   (SE, D, R, FR, SA)

Judas Priest is a middle '70's molten metal band straight from Rock 'n Roll hell. The name Judas implies the ultimate rebel, and the Priest identifies their position. They are self-proclaimed rebel messengers of THE god OF ROCK.

The fans of this bombastic British group sit in a heated frenzie as they listen to their heroes blast unintelligible sounds at decibel levels beyond what the average person could stand.

Similar to other groups of this nature, the members wear black leather signifying their identification with the sado-masochistic movement. They hold Satanic crosses at certain times in their performances, and the audience does likewise.

The album cover of "Sin After Sin" shows the temple of a pagan deity with a skull at the top of the door to the entrance. Also pictured is an obvious temple prostitute lying on the floor at the door of the temple.

This group of storm troopers are not just a critic's bad dream...HEAVY METAL is a genuine sub-culture. How weary is the world of this mess? Obviously not weary enough! Judas Priest still performs their black type of mass.

KANSAS (SE, D, R)

The group Kansas was originally formed in Topeka, Kansas, in the early '70's, but never really got going until 1975 with its debut album "Kansas." This band plays the undistinctive straight-forward Rock in high decibel. Their popularity is strictly due to constant touring.

The album cover of "Audio Visions" pictures stereo earphones personified as nude women with extended tongues. This very provocative depiction has several significant meanings. The extended tongue is symbolic of demon worship and sex. Demons and sex are seen as coming through the music. The album "Point of No Return" pictures a ship falling off of the earth into a sea monster's mouth.

The songs of Kansas fall into three main categories: Advocation of illicit sex, drugs, and rebellion. They were the opening act at Jim Morrison's last concert. Members of Kansas have since become Christians. Let's support their efforts.

KISS (SE, D, R, FR, SA)

Performing evil at its peak, KISS originated in New York City in 1973 behind a charade of Kabuki makeup and barely passable playing. What could have been more of a "hype" than a heretofore unknown band taking makeup to the extreme, blitzkrieging audiences with an arsenal of explosive devices, snow machines, police lights, sirens, rocket-firing guitars, levitating drumkits...and, as if all that wasn't sufficient to disguise their apparent ineptitude. A FIRE-EATING BASS PLAYER!

Despite the obvious "hype," the group became one of the hottest concert bands in the history of Rock. This remains not only a great mystery of Rock criticism, but also the most distressing symptom of the decline of morality around us that can be witnessed.

By the late '70's KISS had experienced worldwide fame. Their concert antics included puking blood while shouting, "We are the god of Rock 'n Roll...we've come to steal your virgin soul." The leather costumes reek with sado-masochistic advocation. Gene Simmons, the one with the extended tongue, confesses an interest in cannibalism. Simmons said in *Circus Magazine* on September 13, 1976, "If God is hot stuff, why is He afraid to have other gods before HIM? I've always wanted to be God." Simmons also said, in *Rolling Stone*, March 25, 1976, "My love techniques are deliciously painful things that make you writhe and groan in ecstasy."

The band berates their audiences with Satanic overtones. Of course, the average KISS fan is a 10 to 13-year-old female. Producer Bob Ezrin's description of KISS is "unfettered evil and sensuality." *Marvel* comics produced a special edition dedicated to KISS with blood samples from the members of the group. They deliberately aimed this edition at 8 to 10 year olds claiming that parents would think it "cute" or a joke. That is what happened! *Marvel's* success then branched out into multifaceted products of KISS paraphernalia.

And, if all of this is not enough, one song "Plaster Caster" should allow anyone to realize the awesome decadence of KISS. The song talks bout Rock groupies (prostitutes who follow bands) who make plaster of Paris replicas of the genitals of Rock musicians and then make love to themselves whenever the desire.

Who knows which part of the KISS hype will affect the millions of teens who emulate them. Will it be the fire-breathing of Gene Simmons? Will it be the sado-masochistic advocations of the entire expression? Will it be the overwhelming violence and rebellion pictured at the concerts? Will it be the Satanic subversion portrayed in the costumes, lyrics and personal lives? Will it be the depiction of false gods such as the force, the sun god, astro travel, the stars, panthesim, and the many others that are flippantly portrayed? Will it be the illicit sex that seems to be the outgrowth of what the members of KISS are teaching? Will it be to follow Gene Simmons who has boasted to have slept with over 1,000 women? Will it be to join the die-hard army of KISS fans who have actually murdered to defend their heros? Will it be falling into the mesmerization of the music to follow the Hitler-like commands of the band? What will be the final effect of the KISS hype?

Ace Frehley, Paul Stanley, Gene Simmons, and Peter Criss, all of whom have made extreme anti-

Christ statements, form the 130-million-dollar-per-year illusion called KISS. Their albums, such as "Love Gun" and "Destroyer"..."Hotter Than Hell," "Dressed to Kill," "Rock and Roll Over," and others strongly project all FIVE of the major themes of Rock music.

KISS is the "pits" of excess in all FIVE areas. They have recently unmasked, but still blast away at Christian principles.

LED ZEPPELIN   (SE, D, R, FR, SA)

Led Zeppelin has been dubbed by the best Rock critics as the greatest Rock 'n Roll band in history. This distinction could only be rivalled by The Rolling Stones or The Who.

The music of Led Zeppelin resembles a Rock and Roll thunderstorm, building to tremendous peaks of violence, and then slipping quickly into calming lulls. The group was the undisputed king of "heavy metal" (loud feedback from guitars).

The "Zep" grew out of the Yardbirds when that group dissolved, leaving Jimmy Page holding the bag to complete their tour commitment. Page himself was a legend in English session work. He contacted old friend and session player, John Paul Jones, who agreed to fill out the defunct Yardbird dates. They were referred to unknowns Robert Plant and John Bonham. This formed the legendary Led Zeppelin.

The name came from the drummer of The Who, Keith Moon, who is reportedly to have said that the group would go down like a "lead balloon."

From the beginning in 1968, this British group concentrated on America. They met with overnight success; consequently, the apocryphal prediction of Moon did not happen. The Led Zeppelin never touched down again.

The "Zep" became one of the biggest concert draws ever. They were able to mix ballad material with heavy metal like no other group had ever accomplished, and this became the distinguishing mark among countless imitators. They had no equality. Their hard bombastic molten metal mixed with delicate precision timing was unprecedented.

The song "Stairway to Heaven," Zeppelin's finest moment, was voted the most popular in all of Rock history. However, this song uses "backward masking" to say, "My sweet Satan, the one who will be the sad one who makes me sad whose power is Satan." I wonder if the voting critics knew that?

Zeppelin's success is in no small measure due to the management skills of one Peter Grant. He is rivalled in his activities only by Col. Tom Parker, Elvis' manager. By restrictive exposure and strategic album releases, Zeppelin established a mystique that allowed them to gain more audience with each tour. In the U.S. tour of 1975, they hit the scene with neon-lit signs, laser beams and 70,000 watts of amplified poison which was at the time the biggest touring sound system in Rock.

Fifteen thousand fans waited over 24 hours for tickets outside New York's Madison Square Garden box office. The same thing happened in Boston, and the ticket demand caused full-scale riot, resulting in an estimated $75,000 damage.

The members of the "Zep" are no stranger to violence themselves. They are on par with other groups in their reputation of destroying hotel rooms, paintings, and electronic equipment (televisions, radios, stereos). They have had motorcycle races in hotel halls and have upheld the groupie (prostitutes of Rock musicians) tradition in no uncertain terms. Robert Plant is described by one U.S. publication as a "self-satisfied carnal gourmet."

Jimmy Page has an overwhelming preoccupation with the occult. He owns Aleister Crowley's infamous Boleskine House on the shores of Loch Ness, Soctland, where Crowley used to perform his black magic rituals. Page also owns an occult bookshop on Holland Street in Kinsington, London, called Equinox.

Robert Plant is deeply involved in the occult, as is Page. Both have been charged with being witches and practicing "black magic."

Drummer John Bonham died from a reaction to a drug used to treat alcoholism, and alcohol itself. Plant blames Page's occult involvement for Bonham's death since it happened at Page's home under questionable circumstances.

Their lyrics portray their basic philosophy. They claim that Rock 'n Roll *IS* sex. Their songs, "Whole Lotta Love" and "Black Dog" portrays an object which explains the force that profoundly affects their audiences...namely *"The* Presence." The album "House of the Holy" pictures nude children climbing stones toward their Rock god.

After the death of drummer John Bonham in September of 1980, the other members of the group announced that without Bonham, Led Zeppelin no longer existed. What was supposed to never get off the ground had finally reached the halls of Rock 'n Roll legend. Their popularity is ever increasing. It is little wonder! The god whom they served so well is probably not through with them yet.

Beware of Led Zeppelin. Beware of everything they touch. They are the major backers of several groups in the current punk scene. Beware!

JOHN LENNON   (SE, D, F, FR SA)

Dr. David Noebel has very accurately called John Lennon "The Marxist Minstrel." He sang songs of atheism, socialism, drugs, revolution, false gods and religions, sex and violence...and hauled millions of dollars to the bank doing it.

Lennon was the prime instigator of the hellish drug culture which has since become a genuine sub-culture. Millions of users who cannot control their habits would have shot John Lennon if they could have. Lennon *was* shot and killed on December 8, 1980, outside his New York apartment by a camp follower who practiced Lennon's philosophy of drugs. Ironic? Unfortunately, his tragic legacy moves on.

John Lennon was born October 9, 1940. This English transplant became the personification of all that Satan desired to do to the human race. Many think him a god. He thought of himself that way. However, the masses only know the media "hype." Very few know what he really stood for.

For example, he once wrote, "Jesus is a garlic-eating, stinking, little yellow greasy fascist bastard Catholic Spaniard." He said, "Of course, I'm wearing a Mao badge ... I'm proud of it." He claimed that the social revolution would grow out of the sexual revolution.

He wrote songs such as the very popular "Imagine," which musically summarizes the history of modern secular man. The lyrics emanate from Nietzsche, Darwin and Marx. "Imagine no heaven ... no hell ... no countries ... no religion ... no possessions ... all the people sharing ... you say I'm a dreamer ... I'm not the only one!!" The entire song reeks of false eastern philosophy while floating in Marxism.

After listening to "Imagine," one can understand how worldwide revolution could also begin to be expressed by the lyrics of the other groups. That is exactly what happened. Mick Jagger of the Rolling Stones got on the band wagon with his song "Street Fighting Man." Elton John followed suit with "Burn Down the Mission."

Oh! We cannot even touch the hem of the garment of what John Lennon did to tear down the systems of authority established by God. Satan found an extremely successful weapon in John Lennon.

After the Beatle break-up, Lennon's recording career ranged from anti-American to anti-Christ and all points in between. He wrote songs such as "Woman is the Nigger of the World," "Mind Games," "Instant Karma," "Imagine," "What Ever Gets You Through the Night"...the titles portray the lyrics.

Lennon was hell-bent on pulling down western society as a whole. He once said, "If one has more than $200 in cash he is a capitalistic creep, deserving destruction." THIS WAS THE BIGGEST SHAM HE EVER PERPETRATED ON THE HUMAN RACE!

Lennon stored millions each year. This Marxist-Leninist revolutionary advocated that "sex, Rock 'n Roll and dope would be the base for the Communist takeover of America."

While trying to take America by hacking at the foundations, Lennon won a lengthy battle with the U.S. Immigration authorities in 1976 and was granted a place in the country he desired to destroy. Why would he want to be in America as opposed to Russia or other communist countries he championed? Simple! To avoid taxes and continue the lifestyle of free love, drugs and Rock 'n Roll.

Now get this!! Lennon ranks as one of the two most successful composers of all of music history. Where are our brains...where are our minds...how can we be so duped and deceived?? Will we let John Lennon live on through the wax that embodies his philosophies? Probably so!

LYNYRD SKYNYRD (SE, D, R)

The group Lynyrd Skynyrd was formed in Jacksonville, Florida, in the early 1970's. Most of the members of the original group attended the same high school and named the band after their gym teacher, Leonard Skinner, who constantly chastened the boys about their hair and manners. By 1973 they had become one of the best and toughest bar bands in the South.

It was in the latter part of '73 that they were "discovered" by Al Kooper. He produced their first album called "Pronounced Leh-Nerd Skinnerd." The album was not representative of the group's ability, but it landed them a spot as the opening act for The Who on the English group's 1973 tour of the United States. From that point they were destined to become one of the top concert draws in the country.

They toured at break-soul pace. They lived on drugs, liquor and maniac antics. They cut the very popular song "Sweet Home Alabama" to answer Neil Young's chauvinistic "Southern Man." Their album "Second Helping" began to center down on what the group was all about. The cover pictures the members of Lynyrd Skynyrd under the covering of the sun god Ra. Other covers pictured "smokes" with skull and crossbones called "Lynyrd Skynyrd Smokes."

After the album "One More for the Road" on October 20, 1977, enroute to Baton Rouge, Louisiana, to play a show, a private plane chartered by the band crashed, killing three of the members of the group and one roadie. This was the end of one of the roughest hard-line Rock bands ever. Their songs depicted sexual freedom, booze, drugs and violence. Their lives became the actual expression of the theme of their music.

It's amazing, but this type doesn't last long! They either die or quit...however, thousands wait to take their place as the puppet on the strings.

PAUL McCARTNEY AND WINGS
(SE, D, R, FR, SA)

Paul McCartney is clearly the most successful soloist of the former Beatles. Born on June 18, 1942, in Liverpool, the ex-Beatle formed his own backup group in 1971. The band was called Wings and was assembled to aid McCartney on tour.

The band was both a success and a failure. Wings could never muster the armies that were assembled by the enemy's use of The Beatles. In this respect they were a failure. However, McCartney continued to turn out the devastating message of the drug subculture. In this respect they were successful.

McCartney has been arrested several times on drug charges, the latest being in 1980 for possession of marijuana. This came upon his arrival in Japan for a Wings concert tour. After spending several days in jail, he was expelled from the country and told he could never return. We could learn a lesson here!

Wings is an undergound term for the first mainline injection of drugs. McCartney said in a *Playboy* interview that neither he nor the rest of the members of the original Beatles believed in God in the slightest.

A little older, and a little more wise, the success of this former Beatle must still be reckoned with.

MEAT LOAF   (SE, D, R, SA)

Meat Loaf was born on September 27, 1947, in Dallas, Texas, with the name Marvin Lee Aday. This young man has become a true Rock 'n Roll spectacle. He is probably the world's largest Rock performer at 6 foot, 260 pounds.

Meat Loaf captured the '70's by storm. He is consistently called Mr. Loaf by the New York Times. The Loaf played the New York bars and even sang lead for Ted Nugent and the crazed Amboy Dukes before landing a spot in a classic '70's cult film entitled "The Rocky Horror Picture Show." At this time he linked up with songwriter Jim Steinman who saw in Meat Loaf a vehicle for his wild science fiction fantasies. The result of all of this was an album produced by Todd Rundgren called "Bat Out of Hell."

The cover for the album pictures a man on a demonic representation of a motorcycle bursting forth from the grave with bats cheering and other demonic depictions. This album featured the famed song "Paradise by the Dashboard Light," which is a musical chronicle of a high school date complete with play-by-play commentary.

Meat Loaf has appeared on several network talk shows espousing his lascivious philosophies with reprobate expression. His antics in performance include everything from simulating a sex act with a microphone and other instruments to the wildest of science fiction farces. This makes his show a major concert draw.

Our combined prayers can change the Loaf's life. Let's try.

THE MOODY BLUES   (SE, D, R, FR, SA)

The Moody Blues was originally formed in 1964 during the height of the British "band boom." It was founded by Denny Laine (now with McCartney and Wings) and two others.

By 1968 Laine had left the group and their popularity began to wane. However, the remaining members hit upon a new thematic approach with the London Symphony. The success was tremendous, and the group stayed with that formula until they became extremely popular with the American Rock underground.

As the group progressed, they became the controversy of "hip" college classes because of their overt symbolism. For example, on the album cover of "In Search of the Lost Chord" birth and death are pictured as happening in hell. A personification of both finds the shaft of the abyss and emerges from darkness to light being changed from despair to sunlight with a face. However, both remain the same essence.

In other words, there is a symbolic picture of The Moody Blues showing their music as hell itself emerging to brighten your day. The title also refers to a chord that if found will enlighten one through the transcendent state of mind it will produce.

This and other albums of like manner have increased the Moody's following to semi-Messianic proportions. Obsessed with their own importance, their lyrics progressed to clichéd cosmic messages.

At the end of 1974 they seemed to feel that they had reached an all-conquering state as a group. Karma maybe? Nevertheless, they began to concentrate on their solo products and have seldom performed as The Moody Blues since. Silent dissolution was the end result of this occultish band.

NAZARETH (SE, R, SA)

The roots of this "Loud 'n Proud" no-frills Rock band are in Dunfermline, Scotland. It was formed in 1969 but did not turn professional until the release of its first album in 1971. They were and are committed to the standard of LOUD, LONG and RAUCOUS.

Produced by ex-Deep Purple members, Nazareth has known several successful singles in the United Kingdom. International success was accrued after the 1975 album "Hair of the Dog." It was in this album that the group allowed their beliefs to become message oriented. This album reflected its contents on a cover full of demons, skulls and dogs.

The dog metaphorically depicts those whose impurity will exclude them from the New Jerusalem. Eastern and Western perspectives place the dog under the idea of ceremonial impurity. Among the ancient Greeks, the dog was the expression of impudence.

There is extreme occultish meaning on the cover of "Hair of the Dog." Someone would have had to be knowledgeable in Satanic symbolism to have depicted the demon expressions found portrayed on it.

Rock critics are agreed that Nazareth is a scornfully low division outfit. Yet, their aggressive stage act adds to their legions. If only they could know the real meaning of Nazareth.

TED NUGENT (SE, R)

Ted "King Gonzo" Nugent, born in 1949 in Detroit, Michigan, has been referred to as The Motor City Madman. There is ample reason for this image. Nugent calls his music "combat rock," and it involves heavy metal thunderings as its main attraction.

Nugent's Amboy Dukes of 1965 were the archetypal garage-band aggregation which, by all laws that governed the "one-shot at fame" Punk Rockers, should have passed into oblivion after their mind blowing pyschedelic anthem "Journey to the Center of the Mind."

Instead, this wax embodied nonsense became a hit single in 1968. Though the Amboy Dukes did eventually pass away, Ted Nugent slugged it out on the solo club circuit becoming crazier each year.

The midwestern media was constantly "chocked full" of Nugent exploits. His antics included jumping from the high amps wearing only a loin cloth and a headband ... shouting pornographic lyrics ... holding guitar feedback battles with members of other Punk and heavy metal groups ... shattering a glass ball by the sound pitch of his guitar ... tearing raw meat apart on stage...and numerous other wild attempts for recognition. These may not have sold Nugent many albums, but they kept his name in the public eye until the times caught up to his persistence.

Although Nugent does not advocate drugs, the Amboy's "Journey to the Center of the Mind" remains on the *Rolling Stones* Psychedelic Top 40. Songs like "Cat Scratch Fever" and "Wang Dang...Poontang" are among Nugent's more successful expressions.

It is clear that Ted Nugent was correct when he said he would not go away. He has now announced that his mind-warping, ear-splitting music will follow the line of mainstream Punk and New Wave.

Nugent declared in a *Circus Magazine* interview that Rock music is a perfect way to vent one's violent tendencies. He said Rock is a vehicle for primal instincts to be released upon other people to demand their responses.

Ted Nugent bills himself as "The Guitar Gunslinger Sent to Blow Your Mind." Ours is blown, Ted. Please stop shooting!

PINK FLOYD   (SE, D, R, FR, SA)

Pink Floyd was launched during the mid-1960's in England as members of several now defunct groups came together for a regular Sunday afternoon gig called "The Spontaneous Underground." It was here that the Floyd built its first following and became the official band of the London underground. Their music consisted of electronic feedback techniques in between Chuck Berry Rock 'n Roll.

In 1966 a young American couple from Tim Leary's Millbrook Institute began to project slides behind the group as they played. This was the development of the first light show to accompany their music.

The name Pink Floyd was adopted from the first names of two Georgia bluesmen, Pink Anderson and Floyd Council. This came from Syd Barrett, founder of the band, who had a working knowledge of the blues.

After the Leary influence Pink Floyd became caught up in the San Francisco psychedelic vibrations. Along with the Crazy World of Arthur Brown and the Soft Machine, Pink Floyd became the archetype of the new wave "psychedelic rock" groups.

In October of 1967 Syd Barrett, who had taken large doses of LSD for inspiration to write the group's material, blew his brain while performing. He had become an acid casualty. The rest of the Floyd remained at the grindstone, however, and became bigger and weirder by the year.

In 1970 they introduced their album "Atom Heart Mother." On May 15 of that year the group performed in concert to promote their album complete with a 50-foot inflatable octopus which arose out of a nearby lake. It was reported by the media that the volume of the speakers killed all of the fish in that same lake. Or maybe they just floated to the surface to hear the band.

In 1972 came the "Dark Side of the Moon" album. This was their magnum opus. The group dealt with stress, death, lunacy, drugs, the occult, and other problems of contemporary society. This album became one of the major sellers of all time. It is still on the American charts. It is probably close to a chart length record, if it has not already attained such.

By this time Pink Floyd's stage show had become a zenith spectacle in concert art. They now possessed an artillery of visual effects, such as crashing aircraft, dry ice, lights, inflatable men with blazing green eyes, and a gong which burst into flames.

The band began to experience real problems after the phenomenal success of "Dark Side," simply due to the fact that they couldn't top the material. However, after several critical disappointments, their album "The Wall" in 1980 has returned the Floyd to somewhat of a credible position.

Pink Floyd has been suprisingly durable. One might wonder why? Easy for the informed. The Floyd had its roots in the drug underground, a very powerful sub-culture. They became heavily involved with Eastern mysticism, astro travel and mind projection. The "Dark Side of the Moon" album cover has nothing but a ray of light shining through a pyramid. They explore the bottomless mysteries of the occult. They sing songs of drugs, sex, rebellion, false religions, and Satan.

They are full-fledged messengers of THE god OF ROCK. For a truth, they were durable, however, they have recently disbanded according to rock reports.

THE PLASMATICS   (SE, D, R)

This band was formed in the late '70's in the heat of the new wave movement. The only thing that is worth mentioning about them has to do with the bizarre on-and-off-stage antics of their lead singer, Wendy O. Williams.

She is definitely a mess! She has been arrested numerous times for lewd and lascivious behavior. She performs nude, simulates sex acts with electronic equipment, massages her lower parts constantly during performances, and advocates the same from all who watch. The album cover of "Beyond the Valley" pictures Wendy bare to the waist in every shot.

Three hours before their Hammersmith Odeon show was to start, the Greater Council of London banned the Plasmatics' British debut on the grounds of safety. "We objected to the blowing up of a car," said a spokesman. (This is part of the act.)

This group is typical of the degradation that the punk and new wave movement is churning up. Anything for a piece of the pie. Wendy O. Williams is certainly trying to cut her share. She recently said, "Why shouldn't I show off my tits? I've got a 38-24-34 figure!" And show them off she does.

The Plasmatics stage performance personifies violence for fans from 10 to 15 years of age.

THE POLICE   (SE, R)

The Police are a new wave English band originally formed around the session man, Andy Summers. The group was one of the first new wave groups to score big in the American market with the hit single "Roxanne."

There is not much to say about them except that they add to the already overcrowded horror of punk. The Police are definitely "arresting" minds.

QUEEN   (SE, D, R, SA)

There is a theory in Rock music. The theory is that when a band of great renown withdraws into a period of inactivity, the vacuum created by the void will be filled by a substitute...usually of lesser talent.

Queen was formed in 1972 around the voice of Freddy Mercury to fill the void created by the foregone Led Zeppelin and David Bowie. They were wild and pretentious, but stylish to a flaw.

"Queen," the name of their first album, which came on the shoulders of a massive EMI promotion campaign, immediately revealed their debt to Led Zeppelin. Heavy metal music had never been fully exploited as a commercial force until Queen took the hard Rock riffs, overlaid them with vocal harmony and commercial melodies, and took off. Remember what we said earlier? We should beware of anything that has to do with Led Zeppelin.

Led Zeppelin was the sledgehammer of molten metal, and Queen became the jackhammer, a more articulate vehicle. They released such strange songs as "Killer Queen," "We are the Champions," and "Tie Your Mother Down."

Queen managed to reach a promotional plateau of outrageousness in 1979. They were going to promote their new single, "Bicycle Races/Fat Bottom Girls." The group invited women to London, especially those with more plump posteriors, to turn out for a nude bicycle race. A staggering number did! The result was a posterior poster and a hit song.

The 1975 album, "A Night at the Opera," is reported to be one of the most expensive albums ever made. The song "Bohemian Rhapsody" contains the line, "Beelezebub has a devil set aside for me." Queen got its name from the "drag overtone" of word "gay." The lead singer, Freddy Mercury, says that he is the devil when on stage. He also says that he probably goes mad several times a year.

Queen's "Get Down and Make Love" advocates the group's sexual philosophy ... namely homosexuality. The group uses the technique of "backward masking" in the song "Another One Bites the Dust." Reversed, the title line repeatedly says, "Begin to smoke marijuana ... begin to smoke marijuana."

The group is now managing itself and in the process is descending further towards the narcissism and self-indulgence which has lurked beneath the surface of its music all along.

Rock critics say that Queen is set for a lengthy stay. It is definitely true that the gay community is out of the woodwork!

THE ROLLING STONES (SE, D, R, FR, S)

One of the most successful and certainly more durable of the British Rock invasion in the '60's is the Rolling Stones. Mick Jagger, the flamboyant superstar, has been at the band's helm since it's inception.

It was Jagger, Keith Richards, Brian Jones, Charlie Watts, and Bill Wyman who first took the Stones on a club circuit with the wildest repertoire of R 'n B yet to be heard in England. This was in January of 1963. They derived their name, The Rolling Stones, from a Muddy Waters song.

The group's innate rebelliousness was sensed by a A&R man, and the group was signed with Decca records. The band was hyped to provide a perfect counterpart for the "clean-cut" Beatles. Ha!

American blues men such as Muddy Waters, Chuck Berry, Bo Diddly and Lightnin Hopkins provided enough material for the band to repackage and take underground to an already "revolution-hungry" English counter-culture.

Their first million-seller entitled "The Last Time," came in 1965 and was penned by Jagger and Richards. By now the Stones had captured the imagination of the young British club scene and the not-so-enthusiastic press. The press began to brand them as dirty, unwashed enemies of decency and society. Naturally, this image only helped to consolidate what was to become a legend.

"I Can't Get No Satisfaction" hit the United States like a storm. This opened the shaft of the abyss and out came the demons of Rock music to make the Stones the loudest messengers of the Enemy to ever pick up a guitar. "Get Off My Cloud"...drug drenched; "Let's Spend the Night Together"...illicit sex; "Their Satanic Majesties"...self-explanatory; and 27 million-selling records to follow. The Stones rank behind only Elvis and the Beatles in the number of worldwide sales.

The antics of the Stones cannot be recorded in the short space we have allotted to their description. The drug busts that surround the members of the group include: March 18, 1965...busted was Mick Jagger for drugs and public urination; February 12, 1967...busted was Jagger, Richards, and Marianne Faithfull. This was the celebrated "drug orgy raid;" May 10, 1967...busted and sent to jail were Jagger and Richards (suspended). May 10, 1967...Bryan Jones busted and given nine months sentence for possession (suspended). May 24, 1968...Jagger and Marianne Faithfull were busted at their home for possession; on and on and on and on and on until February 27, 1977...Keith Richards was busted in Canada for trafficking heroin and cocaine. Richards got off on a suspended sentence and a promise to do a benefit concert for the Canadian Institute of the Blind. (Oh BOOO!)

For sure, the Rolling Stones are the "black" musicians of Rock. They have ranged in their music from the infamous song "Street Fighting Man," which advocated violent revolution, to the theme song of the Satanist churches, namely "Sympathy For the Devil."

One young black man was murdered by the Hell's Angels at a concert at Altamount Speedway in California to the rhythm of "Sympathy For the Devil." What was supposed to be a free concert for the "kids of California" turned into a devil-invoked tragedy for hundreds of loyal fans and death for four.

The Stones have also recorded songs such as the very demonic "Goat's Head Soup," and "Dancin' With Mr. D" (background voodoo incantations and the screams of the demonically possessed).

Mick Jagger is a sexual embarrassment to say the least. Some of the escapades of this deranged man include a stage prop which is a large ballon in the shape of a male phallus. Jagger performs all sorts of illicit sexual advocations with this prop. For example...the attempt to get it in his mouth...a simulated anal intercourse ... and other such bizarre gestures. Of course, the crowd goes wild! Mick struts across the stage wearing mascara and womens clothing trying seriously to protect his image as a practicing bisexual (admitted first sexual experience was homosexual). However, Jagger is a businessman and very smart. He knows what sells!

In 1969 the unbelievably perverted Brian Jones was found dead in his swimming pool. The death was reported as a "misadventure." Jones was a widely-known drug addict. The Stones studied with the Maharishi along with the Beatles in the '60's. The '70's found them still on the scene as enduring fathers of the commercial Rock scene...and the '80's find them still going strong.

Their albums, such as "Black and Blue," allow any person to be aware that they are smart enough to jump on the bandwagon that is pulling the current trends. Sado-masochism is in, and so are the Stones. They are multi-millionaires because of their sexual explicitness, their overindulgence in cocaine and other drugs, their shocking espousal of rebellion and violence, and their outright worship of THE god OF ROCK himself...SATAN. Jagger is called "The Lucifer of Rock," and when he performs, it is certainly obvious!

The only direction that a "stone" can roll...IS DOWNHILL! They have been rolling in this direction for sometime now, and I fear that the bottom is near!

RUSH   (SE, D, R, FR, SA)

The Devil's messengers extra-ordinare...this is the very loud, very long Canadian group Rush. Hailing from Toronto, Rush is a strange mixture of Led Zeppelin and Mr. Spock of Star Trek fame. The group concentrates on science fiction while adorning one of witchcraft's most powerful symbols, a pentagram.

Rush espouses false doctrine of all sorts in their music. For example, a lyrical tale of a battle between the gods Apollo and Dionysus in which the deity Cygnus intervened. The majority of album covers of this group project their major logo . . . the pentagram. The band performs before this logo. It is also on the double set of drums played in concert.

They generally desire for everyone to know who it is they serve.

Rush was formed in the early 70's. Since then they have become enormously popular as they espouse the more darkened messages of THE god OF ROCK. The term "Rush" is rooted drug language no matter what the intent.

R E O SPEEDWAGON   (SE, R)

The straight-ahead Rock group was formed in the middle '70's, and has become one of the nation's largest concert draws. They came from Illinois and have but one formula. Of course...the same as the rest! Hard! Loud! Long! and Bombastic!

This group fits into the same mold as several other stadium rock bands. It is hard for anyone other than loyal fans to tell them apart from Journey, Styx, Foreigner, and Van Halen. It seems that the ones in control of promotion for groups such as this have found a successful niche, and they are *conforming* anyone who wants to emerge on the top into the same mold.

Speedwagon has come out with such brilliant albums as "You Can Tune A Piano But You Can't Tuna Fish." The songs are sick, but the titles are catchy.

The boys in the band "will be boys" at times. They have the reputation of being one of the more destructive groups on the scene today. They damage and destroy hotel and motel property wherever they go. Kevin Cronin recently said, "Living on the brink of disaster at all times is what Rock 'n Roll is all about." This statement pretty well sums up the philosophy of these manipulated servants of their god.

One of their more successful albums is "High-Infidelity." An affair is advocated and depicted. What problem, you say?? Just ruined lives! No problem, just broken homes! On the album cover of "Nine Lives," cat women are seen in chains.

Speedwagon has been bludgeoned by critics, but every concert is sold out. They are faceles and nameless . . . and managed in such a manner as to withstand the agonies and the ecstasies of the road.

What energy! If only they could know our Lord.

SANTANA   (SE, D, R, FR, SA)

Carlos Santana launched the group that bore his name during the late '60's. Carlos was born in Autlan, Mexico, in 1947 and grew up playing guitar in the red light district of Tijuana. He moved to San Francisco during the time of the Haight-Asbury "flower power" explosion. The group appeared at the celebrated Woodstock in 1969, and from that point forward was successful.

Santana had two back-to-back hits in 1970 entitled "Evil Ways," and "Black Magic Woman." This should be some indication of the philosophy of Carlos Santana. The album "Abraxas" relates to one of the more powerful demons in occult literature. Santana later disbanded the original group and embraced the teachings of the noted guru Sri Chinmoy. Through his new teaching he adopted a new name...Devidip. The album "The Festival," pictures a roaring lion walking about on human legs. There are many hidden messages in the face of the lion. Notice I Peter 5:8...and see who this is!

Carlos Santana lost much of his commercial appeal when he and other disciples followed Chinmoy down a completely different road. He sings of free love, devotion to pantheism, surrender to alien gods, rebellion in the name of peace, drugs, and Satan.

This was a flower band that did not make the cut. Maybe the '80's will not be forced to experience Carlos Santana (Devidip) and his strange philosophy.

SEAL AND CROFTS   (FR)

Jim Seals and Dash Crofts met in junior high school in Texas. They first attained some taste for the music business when they played on the middle '50's tune "Tequila" by the Champs.

They were converted to the Baha'i religion in the '60's and began to emerge as crusading disciples of the enlightened few.

The new duo sound projected by Seals and Crofts immediately shot them up the charts. The '70's saw tremendous success for the duo, but it is not easily explained by Rock critics. It is easy enough for the Christian, however. The boys would not perform unless they had the privilege to share their Baha'i faith at the end of a concert.

THE god OF ROCK used them for a while to cause those fans who would listen to consider the idea of other gods and other religions alien to their own.

It briefly worked, although their success has been tempered in present times. They are called "the super-whimps of the '70's."

THE SEX PISTOLS   (SE, D, R)

All hype aside, the Sex Pistols stand as the most important band of the '70's as far as the "Punk" scene is concerned. They almost single-handedly launched this bizarre trend in Great Britain.

The clear beginnings of "Punk" were American in root, but because of the revolutionary state of Britain, the door was open for the explosion of the new wave music.

The Sex Pistols were outrageously rude, crude, uncouth, unmannered, spoiled, demented, sick, pigged-out, gross, vulgar, and incredibly raunchy. They quickly grabbed the title for being "Punks" all-time most dangerous band. Things would happen in the clubs where they played that only the very stupid or very large would brave.

The members of the group began to change their names to fit their personal philosophies. The entire "Punk" scene followed suit. Some of the members of the Pistols were Johnny Rotton (so named because of his rotten teeth) and Sid Vicious. These names described what the boys were like.

The Pistols sang songs such as "Anarchy in the U.K." and the infamous "God Save the Queen." This song was so gross that is was banned from all forms of media in England. The Pistols had trouble with every record label to which they were signed. One label reportedly gave them $200,000 just to get lost! Then they signed with **Warner Brothers** who had the weird philosophy that if the Pistols made money, nothing they could do — as raunchy as it might be — would be sufficiently offensive to let them go. Good for Warner Brothers!! However, in 1979 with only one album on the American label, Sid Vicious died of an overdose of drugs after being arrested for the supposed murder of his girlfriend. The Sex Pistols opened the door for other demented groups to flood England and America's fertile soil.

The Pistols were formed in 1975 by a clothes tradesman, **Malcom McClaren,** who owned an erotic clothes shop called Sex in London's Kings Road. The members of the group were found hanging around the sex shop premises. They had never sung, but could pose and sneer well enough to satisfy the imagination of their deranged manager who saw in them a way to crack the American "Punk" world.

Their songs express the gutter vile of their minds and the nihilistic anger of their streets. They were given the reputation as the band that would make Rock 'n Roll dangerous again. Their music, if that is a proper term, was hard, loud and unintelligible. The Pistols came in shooting lyrical bullets at the open minds of punkers, and while they didn't shoot long, they did hit some targets and made a lasting impact on an already hellish phenomenon known as PUNK ROCK

ROD STEWART   (SE)

Rod Stewart was born in 1945 in London. After aspiring to be a soccer player, he drifted into music almost by accident. While bumming around with British folk-singer Wizz Jones, Stewart began singing for a series of R&B based bands. He wound up joining the Jeff Beck Group in 1968 as a vocalist. He then formed the band Faces, and later changed the billing to Rod Stewart and Faces. Afterward, he was on his way to national recognition.

Then came the hit single "Maggie Mae," which portrayed a young college lad having a summer fling in the bed of an older woman. Following was hit after hit until Stewart has surpassed even Mick Jagger as the sex-symbol superstar of the '70's.

The 1979 single "Do Ya Think I'm Sexy" became the fastest selling record in Warner Brothers' history. Obviously, somebody thought he was! Stewart would perform the song dressed in skin tight pants while showing his posterior to the audience in a sickening display of acrobatics.

Stewart's love exploits have been highly publicized. His affairs with Hollywood glamour girls identify his person almost as much as his music. In the song "Tonight's the Night" Stewart requests the young girl to "spread her wings so he can come inside."

He relies heavily upon a "bisexual" expression in his performances. He has been reported as saying, "I want to be attractive to men, also." Stewart has proven that sex sells!

His stamina has been incredible, however he continues to lead his followers astray.

STYX (SE, D, R, FR, SA)

This group was formed in Chicago in 1970 from a bar band called Tradewinds. They fall into the same mold as several other concert crowd bands that built their reputation on incessant touring and repertoire that borrowed heavily from the flashy British rock hypes extraordinare. Not much can be said about them other than they seem to serve their god quite well.

Their name came from the mythological river that flows through Hell. In their album "Cornerstone" what is depicted on the cover seems to be a representation of Christ as the head of the corner of a rectangular building, not a pyramid. The apex or top stone of the pyramid represents the power or the deity behind the pyramid. Since the pyramids were built in a sun-god worshipping, idolatrous, demonical culture, it is highly unlikely they were built to honor God.

Styx is selling out concerts all over the nation. They have been manipulated into believing that they are gods and can name their desire! Right now, in the Rock music scene, they can and do.

The River Styx is flowing — crystal balls and astrological charts on their album covers tell all who purchase what the group stands for! Loud, heavy, teeth-shattering, deafening, metallic, bombastic, and unintelligible are only a few words that describe their style.

THE 10CC   (SE, D, R)

10CC was formed in England around the former members of the group, The Mindbenders. The band hit the American market in 1975 with the hit "The Things We Do For Love." Graham Gouldman, a successful writer over a long period of time, catapulted 10CC to national acclaim.

The name 10CC came from the average amount of sperm in one male ejaculation. This should give anyone who knows the facts an idea as to what the group stands for.

Their music is decidedly different from most of the English heavy metalers. The press has actually critized this group for their "calculated pop" sound.

In other words, they are what is known as a middle-of-the-road Rock band. Their songs are easy and sexually oriented. This is a lyric that can be understood and received into the mind. Really, this type is somewhat more dangerous.

10CC...man what will the bands come up with next???

URIAH HEEP   (SE, D, R, SA)

This very heavy metal group was formed in 1970 and shamelessly plagiarized the metallic sounds of the Led Zeppelin. They were even called "the bastard offspring of Deep Purple."

Uriah Heep is one of the most critically dumped on bands ever. In fact, one critic wrote of their first album, "Very 'eavy...very 'umble. If this group makes it, I'll have to commit suicide." Not only did they make it, but they became one of the mainstays of the '70's.

Their roots are English and their music is like an earthquake. With the album "Demons and Wizards," which came in 1972, their pace began to pick up and the Heep was rolling.

The bassist, Gary Thain, was severely shocked while performing on stage in Dallas, Texas, in 1974. He was later found dead of an overdose of pills.

This heavy metal copy has experienced internal feuding from its unnecessary inception. Their latest album pictures the most eerie depiction of what the devil must look like that this writer has ever seen.

Although this group has dedicated much wax to their god, if you've heard one Heep record, you've heard them all. By the way, no one knows what happened to the previously-mentioned critic!

VAN HALEN (SE, DR, SA)

These arrogant, self-proclaimed gods of metal music began in California during the mid '70's. Two brothers, Eddie Van Halen and Alex Van Halen, were known by as many names as they could think of in order to remain fresh on the California club scene.

They were, unfortunately, discovered in a Hollywood Rock club in 1977, and their first album sold two million copies almost immediately. This proved that the manipulators of Rock had found the formula that was selling. Van Halen went in with the other stadium Rock groups and produced a loud, long, powerful, ear-bursting, teeth-shattering, yet overwhelmingly popular sound (it could never be called music).

These arrogant young men actually demand from Rock promoters everything they want...EVERYTHING, and get it, or they will not play. A writer for *Rolling Stone* magazine said, "After spending several days on the road with Van Halen, I've seen enough nude women and heard enough morning anecdotes to fuel an article about porn Rock."

Some of the reported stories about this haughty band would actually cause one to disbelieve what he was hearing. Most would probably say, "Oh!! That couldn't be true!" But, friend, whatever you hear about them has probably come *from* them. They are proud of the devastation and destruction they can cause. They treat their audience like dirt. They do not care what happens to them...from being beaten up, passing out, overdosing, to rioting. The band incites harm and calls hell up to perform it. They are called stormtroopers, and their music is called combat Rock.They are a promoter's bad dream and the critic's nightmare. They are seeking to be macho deities of metal Rock, and at the time of this writing, they are!

Young people, if you only knew what David Lee Roth (the lead singer) thinks about you...you might not think so much of him! Van Halen is nothing but four guys who can walk on stage and make thousands of young people do practically anything they say. Their demands have included everything from disrobing to tearing down buildings.

"...and He (God) will put down all who try to raise themselves before Him." One of these days, Van Halen's knees will bow, and their tears will begin to flow. They will cry for the rocks and the mountains to fall upon them and cover them from the wrath that will certainly be their plight if they continue to serve THE god OF ROCK in the manner they do now!

THE WHO (SE, DR, FR,SA)

The Who was formed in London in 1963. They have survived because of their innate ability to be destructive. They have managed to become one of Rock's all-time great concert-drawing bands.

Their music did not follow the already overflowing scene of R&B but identified more with the Mod crowd. They became recognized when the members began to smash and destroy their instruments at the end of each show. This was, at the time, very dramatic, expensive, and probably symbolic of what was to come.

The Who began their destructive touring in the late '60's until Pete Townsend hit upon the door opener that increased their popularity to superstar status. It was the Rock opera "Tommy." "Tommy" was a metaphoric mockery of Jesus Christ. This so-called opera depicted everything from a surrealistic crucifixion to scenes of child molesting.

"Tommy" was unprecedented in its success but took its toll on the writers. During the mid '70's, it appeared that The Who was on the verge of breaking up. However, it was at this time that Townsend regrouped under the influence of eastern mysticism. He was greatly affected by the teachings of Meher Baba and became one of the strongest proponents of the faith.

The Who was known for burning equipment, both on stage and off, setting off smoke bombs in hotels, and general destruction of all sorts... and this was in the early days. It was reported on one tour that the group destroyed over $35,000 worth of personal hotel property to celebrate the birthday of one of the members.

Pete Townshend declares that Baba is Christ. In a *Rolling Stone* interview, Townshend reported chanting the Hindu "Om," and going into a trance through which he heard the roar of billions of humans screaming. This frightened Pete, and he said that what he had probably heard was hell itself.

The Who drummer, the late Keith Moon, was heralded as being the craziest of the group by far. From public excretion to public exposure, Moon's antics are almost unprecedented. He has driven cars into swimming pools; taken a hatchet and chopped up hotel furniture out of boredom; taken as many as twenty amphetamines at a time; and chased nude young women from his room into lobbies of major hotels and had sex with them on the floor. Moon finally died of an overdose of anti-alcoholism tablets.

In *The Book of Rock Lists*, The Who ranks number one in all-time destructive stage acts. They sing songs of sex, such as their hit "Mama's Got a Squeeze Box" (self-explanatory). They espouse false religions, violence, rebellion, and shades of demonism. The album "Hooligans" features destroyed property. The album "Magic Bus" features their philosophy of drugs. Their message is bombastic and strong. The Who is a so-called institution in the annals of Rock history.

Roger Daltry, lead singer, has an eight-foot replica of a genital in the yard of his home in Sussex.

To many parents the name, The Who, fits their knowledge of who the group is. They say, "Who?" Not the kids! They know!

ZZ TOP   (SE, D, R)

A southern blues boogie band that made it big, the ZZ was formed by Billy Gibbons in 1970. Other members include Dusty Hill and Frank Beard. They have become a fantastically successful straight-ahead heavy rock band. They have been responsible for one of the most excessive touring aggregations ever seen in the concert world. They went on tour with live buffalos, vultures, cactus, and a stage shaped like Texas. It took several tractor trailer rigs to move the equipment. The group wanted to bring Texas to the people elsewhere.

The ZZ has reached superstar status through good management, tight playing, and right moves. One of the members is into eastern mysticism, one into nothing, and the other avidly searching for the truth. The name came from Zig Zag roll-your-own papers used to roll marijuana smokes. Their logos have included skull and crossbones, and other interesting items.

They sing songs about whorehouses, booze, the blues, and friendly frenzy. Their albums include such titles as "El Loco" and "Fandango." The song "Tube Snake Boogie" tells of girls who do the tube snake boogie (sexual intercourse). The song "Pearl Necklace" tells of the insertion of foreign objects into the body for sexual purposes.

There is no doubt about the fact that ZZ can pack a stadium. One of the foremost critics of Rock says, "I have seen the best of Rock 'n Roll, and it *is* ZZ Top." It looks like they are here for a lengthy stay.

Their popular song in 1974 entitled "La Grange" is about the same whorehouse that is now being glorified in the movie "The Best Little Whorehouse in Texas."

A little ahead of your time, huh, ZZ?

What a victory it would be if the Christian community organized to pray for the salvation of these individuals and many others not mentioned. They need to know the peace that only Jesus can bring to a life. The rock music industry is prone to devour it's own. Let's begin to pray and see what happens.

CHAPTER SIX
THE PROOF OF THE PUDDIN'
(Lyrics, Facts, Quotes and Tracks)

For nearly twenty years record companies have been lining their pockets with billions by stealing the innocence of our children and replacing it with vile perversions found in the lyrics of Rock 'n Roll.

Today, the lyrics in over one hundred million-selling records are so corrupt that they cannot, by law, be played on radio or other forms of public media. Yet, these same songs *ARE* being broadcast into the homes of most teenagers by stations who are in clear violation of existing federal law, and through mental and spiritual poison incorporated in the wax itself.

Because of the loud volume of the music, most parents force their children to retreat to their rooms where, in many cases, the gods of Rock are plastered on every space of wall available. It would seem that some teens have literally made a pagan temple or shrine out of their own bedrooms. Parents need not fear their children running off to serve some idol or worship some false god. They don't have to! They just go to their faulty classroom (bedroom) and learn about drugs, promiscuity, rebellion, homosexuality, beastiality, sadomasochism, incest, necrophilia and other perversions.

Who is the teacher? Where do they hear this trash? Why, from their Rock idols! Their minds become polluted and contaminated because of the message of the music!

The problem has reached such monstrous proportions that an entire generation of children is in grave danger. We are actually only one generation from total depravity expressed. Unless we change our tune (pardon the pun), we will live in a music-inspired, lust-motivated, totally hedonistic society. The end result will be a perverted national sham that is unthinkable.

Today's young people are being drowned in a cesspool that is not of their own making. It is high time people became aware of what is happening and man the lifeboats. The following information is intended to reveal at a glance something about what is seemingly going unnoticed by parents, pastors, and teachers. We must put a permanent end to the garbage that is infecting our teens and children. I have heard, "Prove it to me!" many times. All right... here's proof! Let's look at some LYRICS, FACTS, QUOTES and TRACKS.

LYRICS

AC ⚡ DC
Album: Back in Black
Subject: Vehicle to hell is Rock music
Song: Hells Bells
"I'm a rollin' thunder pourin' rain,
I'm comin' on like a hurricane.

My lightning's flashing across the sky,
You're only young, but you're gonna die!
Nobody's puttin' up a fight ...
I got my bell, I'm gonna take you to hell,
I'm gonna get ya, Satan, get ya, HELLS BELLS!"

OZZY OSBOURNE
Album: Diary of a Madman
Subject: Demon possession
Song: Diary of a Madman
"A sickened mind and spirit,
the mirror tells me lies.
Could I mistake myself for someone
who lives behind my eyes?
Will he escape my soul,
or will he live in me?
Is he tryin' to get out or tryin' to enter me?"

IRON MAIDEN
Album: Number of the Beast
Subject: Setting forth Satan as God
Song: Number of the Beast
"Woe to you, of earth and sea ...
For the devil sends the beast with wrath;
'Cause he knows the time is short.
Let him who has understanding
Reckon the number of the beast;
For it is a human number,
It's the number six hundred and sixty-six.
Satan's work is done!
666 the number of the beasts!
Sacrifice is going on tonight!"

BLACK SABBATH
Album: Master of Reality
Subject: Satan's rivalry against God
Song: Lord of this World
"Your soul is ill, but you will not find a cure.
Your world was made for you by someone above;
But you chose evil ways instead of love.
You made me master of the world where you exist.
The soul I took from you was not even missed.
Lord of this world ...
Evil possessor ...
Lord of this world ...
He's your confessor now!
You think you're innocent, you've nothing to fear!
You don't know me, you say, but isn't it clear?
You turn to me in all your wordly greed and pride ...
But will you turn to me when it's your turn to die?"

ALICE COOPER
Album: Billion Dollar Babies
Subject: Necrophilia (having sex with a corpse)
Song: I Love the Dead
"I love the dead before they're cold,
Their bluing flesh for me to hold,
While friends and lovers mourn your silly grave,
I have other uses for you, darling.
We love the dead...."

AC ⚡ DC
Album: Back in Black
Subject: Sexual intercourse/oral sex
Song: You Shook Me All Night Long

"She was a fast machine,
She kept her motor clean,
She was the best damned woman that I ever seen.
Knockin' me out with those American thighs...
Takin' my little share had me fighting for air;
She told me to come ... I was already there.
'Cause the walls start shakin',
The earth was quakin',
You weren't fakin' ... when you
Shook me all night long."

KISS
Album: Love Gun
Subject: Plaster casts of male genitals for
          masturbation
Song: Plaster Caster
"My baby's gettin' anxious,
The hour is gettin' late ...
The night is almost over,
She can't wait!
Things are complicating,
My love is in her hands,
and now there's no waitin'...
She understands!
The plaster's gettin' harder,
She's the collector --
She wants me all the time ...
To inject her."

THE WHO
Album: Face Dances
Subject: Sexual intercourse

Song: You Better You Bet
"I've got your body right now on my mind,
But I've drunk myself blind...
You welcome me with open arms and open legs,
You better bet your life,
Or my love will cut you like a knife."

PRINCE
Album: Dirty Mind
Subject: Sexual intercourse
Song: Dirty Mind
"...Whenever I'm around you, babe,
I get a dirty mind.
I just wanna lay you down in my daddy's car,
If you got the time.
I'll give you some money ... to buy a dirty mind,
But, hon, you got me on my knees ...
Won't you please let me lay you down, down, down?"

AC ⚡ DC
Album: Back in Black
Subject: Oral sex
Song: Givin' the Dog a Bone
"Should take her down easy, goin' down to her knees,
Goin' down to the devil, down, down to 90 degrees.
She's drivin' me crazy, till my ammunition is dry...
Givin' a dog a bone.
She's got the power of union,
Only licks when it's hot ...
If she likes what you're doin',
She'll lick you a lot.
Givin' the dog a bone."

DEVO
Album: We are Devo
Subject: Masturbation
Song: Praying Hands
"You got your left hand.
You got your right hand.
The left hand's diddling,
While the right hand goes to work ...
You got praying hands,
They pray for no man ...
Okay -- relax ...
Assume the position,
Go into doggie submission."

QUEEN
Album: News of the World
Subject: Oral sex (homo/bisexuality)
Song: Get Down, Make Love
"Get down, make love ... you take my body.
I give you heat, you say you're hungry...
I give you meat. I suck your mind,
You blow my head, make love inside your bed...
Everybody, get down and make love...."

DR. HOOK
Album: Sloppy Seconds
Subject: Sado-masochism/Necrophilia
Song: Freakers' Ball
"C'mon, babies, grease your lips
Put on your hats and swing your hips.
Don't forget to bring your whips...
We're goin' to the freakers' ball.

Black ones, white ones, yellow ones and red ones,
The greatest of the sadists and the masochists, too.
Screamin', 'Please hit me and I'll hit you.'
We're goin' to the freakers' ball...."

LINDA CRAWFORD
Album: I'm Yours
Subject: Male ejaculation/sexual intercourse
Song: Shoot Your Best Shot
"And you want all the love I've got?
If you want me,
If you need me...
Gotta have me,
Believe me, I've got a lot.
If you want me,
If you need me...
Gotta have me,
... come on --shoot it, baby!"

DR. HOOK
Album: Rising
Subject: First sexual experience of virgin girl
Song: That Didn't Hurt Too Bad
"I'm gonna handle you like a baby,
I'm gonna love you like you never knew...
And it'll be everything and more,
Than you ever thought it could,
And you're gonna be so good.
Ohhh...that didn't hurt too bad, now did it?"

PINK FLOYD
Album: Dark Side of the Moon

Subject: Drug Abuse
Song: Breathe
"...For as long as you live and high you fly,
But only if you ride the tide;
And balanced on the biggest wave...
You race toward an early grave...."

ALAN PARSONS
Album: The Alan Parsons Project
Subject: Experimentation with Black Magic
Song: Maybe a Price to Pay
"Something's wrong in this house today,
While the Master was riding,
His servants decided to play.
... there's evil brewing, getting out of control,
Something unrighteous is possessing my soul...
Might be too much Sun, too much in the Air,
Whatever's happening, nobody else is aware...
Something's wrong in this house today,
There may be a price to pay."

STEELY DAN
Album: Gaucho
Subject: Heroin Addiction
Song: Time Out of Mind
"Tonight when I chase the Dragon,
The water will change to wine,
And the silver will turn to gold.
Time out of Mind.
I'm holding the mystical stone.
It's direct from Lasa

Where people are rolling in the 'snow'
Far from the world we know."

PINK FLOYD
Album: Animals
Subject: Satan's Followers
Song: Sheep
"The Lord is my shepherd, I shall not want.
He makes me down to lie.
Through pastures green he leadeth me
The silent waters by.
With bright knives he releaseth my soul.
He maketh me to hang on hooks in high places,
He converteth me to lamb cutlets.
For lo, he hath great power and great hunger...."

CROSBY, STILLS AND NASH
Album: Crosby, Stills and Nash
Subject: Universalism
Song: Cathedral
"...I'm flying in Winchester cathedral,
All religion has to have its day.
Expressions on the face of the Savior,
Made me say, I cannot stay!
Open up the gates of the church
And let me out of here!
Too many people have died in the name of Christ
For anyone to heed the call.
Too many people have died in the name of Christ
That I can't believe it all...."

DEAD KENNEDYS
Album: The Dead Kennedys
Subject: Murder
Song: I Kill Children
"God told me to skin you alive...
I kill children,
I love to see them die,
I kill children,
To make their mothers cry.
I crush them under my car,
And I love to hear them scream.
I feed them poison candy,
And spoil their halloween...
I kill children."

SUPERTRAMP
Album: Even in the Quietest Moments
Subject: Eastern Mysticism
Song: Babaji
"All of my life I felt that you were listening,
Watching for ways to help me stay in tune,
Lord of my dreams, although confusion,
Keeps trying to deceive...
What is it that makes me believe in you?
Babaji, oh won't you come to me?
Won't you help me face the music?"

ELTON JOHN
Album: Goodbye Yellow Brick Road
Subject: Masturbation
Song: Jamaica Jerk-Off
"...It's no good living in the sun

Playing guitar all day,
Boogalooin' with my friends
In some erotic way...
Come on, Jamaica,
Everybody say...
We're happy in Jamaica,
Do Jamaica jerk-off that way."

ELTON JOHN
Album: Goodbye Yellow Brick Road
Subject: Lesbianism
Song: All the Girls Love Alice
"All the young girls love Alice,
Tender young Alice they say,
Come over and see me...
Come over and please me...
Alice, it's my turn today."

These lyrics represent only a smattering of what lies in wait for those who purchase this trash. Some of the following facts will further demonstrate the horror that is upon us!

FACTS

Jerry Rubin, author of *Do It* (The Communist Manifesto of the '70's), said, "We see sex, rock and roll, and dope as a part of the Communist plot to take over America." It is reported that his book was a declaration of war between the generations. He called for the kids to leave their homes, burn down their schools and create a new society upon the ashes of the old. Rubin also called for the killing of parents as a protest against the establishment. He sees Rock music as the beginning of the revolution. He declares that Rock caused the sex and drug revolution and these, in turn, allowed Marxism to enter our country unchallenged. "We've combined youth, music, drugs, and rebellion with treason —and that's a tough combination to beat."[1]

Aristotle once said, "Emotions of any kind are produced by melody and rhythm. Music has the power to form character, whether melancholy, effeminacy, or abandonment."[2]

Dr. Joyce Brothers stated, "Meaningless noise destroys the ability to relax, reflect, study, pray, meditate, and, in fact, prepares people for riot, civil disturbance and revolution."[3]

Dr. Benard Saibel, a child guidance expert for the State of Washington declared, "Hysteria experienced by teens at Rock concerts caused them to become frantic, hostile, uncontrollable, screaming, unrecognizable beings."[4]

America is obsessed with air and water pollution, but somehow has failed to recognize the mental and spiritual pollution which threatens its most precious natural resource — its youth! If one listens to the radio for even a short length of time, he must conclude that young people are hooked on raw sex, pot, and birth control pills. However, the poison is so subtle that most parents have paid little attention to the harmful effects that it is having upon their children.

Edward Hunter said in his book *Brainwashing,* "Noise, lights, music, reflexes, nerve jamming, and a form of neurosis are being used by the Communists to invade the privacy of our children's minds and render them mentally incompetent."[5]

Dimitri Tiomkin, a famous composer, said in an *LA Herald Examiner* article, "Now, in our popular music, at least, we seem to be reverting to savagery. And the most dramatic indication of this is the number of occasions in recent years when rock concerts have erupted into riots."[6]

Riots and other forms of violence go hand in glove with the Rock concert scene. For example, in 1965 in Jacksonville, Florida, there were 6,700 youth who were worked into a screaming frenzy by Jim Morrison and the Doors. The police reported the young people as having sex with one another in the open, fighting and stabbing one another, and destroying property. The authorities said the crowd was like a herd of stampeding cattle.

The same thing was occurring all over the globe. In Long Beach, California, there were 4,000 fans who broke into a riot, damaging thousands of dollars worth of property and hospitalizing hundreds. This happened in 1965, along with the first San Francisco riot in which 10,000 fans destroyed automobiles and shops, and injured scores of people. The people attributed the destruction to the strange powers of the Rock musicians. The same year brought yet another riot to San Francisco in which 3,500 were so wild that the National Guard and police dogs were ordered into the area. There were stompings, stabbings, maulings, and shootings. The police attributed the cause to the Rock group The Animals. It was reported that the group wound the crowd up so tight, it snapped!

Also, in 1965 at the Los Angeles Sports Arena, there were 15,000 fans in mass hysteria. The reports described girls ripping off their clothes, attacking one another, and doing exactly what the musicians told them to do. There were many hospitalizations and much damage to property. The authorities attributed the cause to the Rock group The Rolling Stones. The same thing happened in Vancouver, Canada, Melborne, Australia, and even Beirut, Lebanon . . . all in 1965. These riots were caused by a variety of different groups!

This type of scene is still happening! One would think that the average person could see the terrible danger, and do something to stop it! We have done only one thing . . . *THE OSTRICH TRICK!* Concerts are big business . . . big money, and the righteous have been warned to leave them alone!

The danger really came to the forefront of national attention as a result of the highly publicized "free" concert given by The Rolling Stones at Altamont Speedway in San Francisco, California. What was supposed to be a celebration for the kids of California turned into a disorganized orgy involving sex, drugs, and death. In the darkness, as Mick Jagger performed "Sympathy for the Devil," a young black girl was stabbed to death at the foot of the bandstand by The Hell's Angels who had been hired as bodyguards for The Stones. Four other people lost their lives in this hell-invoked fury called a Rock concert.

These are only a few of the facts that surround the indescribable terror that can develop during a Rock performance. Please consider the absolute impossibility to record everything that has happened since the concert scene had its inception. Only several have been mentioned, and all of them in the 1960's. To bring this phenomenon current, let me gently jog your memory. The year — 1980! The place — Cincinnati's Riverfront Stadium. The scene — a concert featuring The Who. Eighteen thousand pressed toward the ticket counters. When the gate was opened, throngs of youth rushed madly forward suffocating and crushing 11 precious kids to death. Hundreds were injured and hospitalized because of the crowd's frenzy. And what did the Rock group think about it? They said they were sorry, and that they would try to work on their security. That's nice! Try telling that to one of the parents!

Also, in 1980 in Dallas, Texas, a riot occurred in a ticket line after scores of people had spent the night waiting for tickets to a ZZ Top concert. Thousands of dollars in damage was caused as people were pushed through large plate glass windows. Sounds like just the place to be, huh? That is, if you are looking for a trip to the hospital!

There are literally hundreds of recorded incidents similar to the ones just described. Mr. Tiomkin, the composer, made his statement concerning riots at Rock concerts in 1965. As has already been mentioned . . . you'd think we'd get the message eventually!

Henry David Thoreau predicted in 1854 that music would someday destroy England and America. It appears, unless something is done, he might be right![7]

According to Dr. David Noebel, the origins of Rock go to the deep South, and from there can be directly traced to Africa where it was used to incite warriors to such a frenzy that by nightfall their neighbors were cooked in carnage pots. "The music is a designated reversion to savagery," says Noebel.[8]

Gene Lees, a noted Jazz critic states, "Rock is the cause of America's terrible problems with its young people. It is destructive, negative, and nihilistic."[9]

According to John Phillips of the Mamas and Papas, it is a simple thing to control or create audience hysteria. He admitted, "We can create crowd hysteria by controlling the sequence of rhythms very carefully. We know how to do it, and most other groups do too."[10]

Not only can the groups create audience hysteria, they could probably put Dale Carnegie out of business with their unbelievably seductive sales approaches. There are literally hundreds of drug-pushing discs that are being constantly consumed by our young people. The sales pitch is loud and long. And the really sad part is . . . IT WORKS! Listen to Grace Slick of the Jefferson Starship . . .

"Handfuls of rock groups have been liberated by the use of LSD. We all use drugs and condone the use of drugs for everyone. Let the people groove . . . let them ball on the grass in the open! I dig watching people have sex."[11]

Grace Slick is not the only one with this philosophy. If the truth were known, probably 99 and 9/10's of the rest of the Rock world believes and advocates the same thing. Frank Zappa of The Mothers of Invention said, "Society's major hangups could be cured by a drug and sexual openness."[12]

Some of the many songs that have become drug-pushing enticements are: "Heroin" by The Velvet Underground (Lou Reed, formerly of this group is famous for "shooting up" on the stage during concert performances); "Junker's Blues" by Michael Bloomfield; "The Needle and the Damage Done" by Lynyrd Skynard; "The Pusher" by Steppenwolf; "Cocaine" by Jackson Browne; "Get Off My Cloud" by The Rolling Stones; "Journey to the Center of the Mind" by Ted Nugent; "In A-Gadda-da-Vida" by The Iron Butterfly; "She's a Rainbow" by the Rolling Stones; "Strawberry Fields Forever" by The Beatles; "Room Full of Mirrors" by Jimi Hendrix; "Rainey Day Woman" by Bob Dylan; "White Rabbit" by The Jefferson Airplane; ad infinitum ad nauseum, as David Noebel says.

These are several titles from The Psychedelic Top 40 compiled by *The Book of Rock Lists* which contains the all-time best selling drug saturated discs. One has only to check any music store to see the quantity of underground advocations embodied in wax that invite young people to take off on a "high." It is obvious that dangerous drugs cannot be sold in the same manner as apple pie and vanilla ice cream. How then is the message to be spread? Simple — through the vehicle of Rock music! How did what was once a ghetto problem become the major downfall of so many youth all across America? Rock musicians put wheels to the words! Please do not be deceived . . . herein lies the culprit!

Paul McCartney said, " . . . if politicians would use LSD, there would be no more war, poverty or famine."[13]

A House Committee on Crime said in a report called *Illicit and Dangerous Drugs,* "At least one-half of the Top 40 records present a constant secret message to the whole teenage world to drop out, turn on, and groove with chemicals." This report was made in 1969. Rock music has been the vehicle used to destroy an entire generation and set the stage for the almost certain destruction of the next. THE DOWNBOUND TRAIN IS CERTAINLY GAINING MOMENTUM!![14]

Rock ridicules religion and morality while, at the same time, glorifies drugs, sexual promiscuity and rebellion. The sexual revolution began when diamond needles slipped between the grooves and belittled what was intended for man's ultimate pleasure within the framework of God's perfect design. A mockery was made of the marriage bed, and God's creation was perverted and packaged for consumption. THE god OF ROCK sure knew how to "hit home."

The manager of the Rolling Stones said, "Rock IS sex. You have to hit teenagers in the face with it!" Jagger is a master at hitting kids in the face with perversion. He has been doing it for years, and is still going strong.[15]

In a late 1960's interview with Time Magazine, the members of the Jefferson Airplane said, "The stage is our bed, and the audience is our broad. We're not entertaining; we're making love!"[16]

The *late* Jim Morrison screamed at a concert, "Man!!! I'd like to see a little nakedness around here!!! Grab your old ladies and make love!! There are no laws here . . . there are NO RULES!!" He was later arrested for lewd and lascivious behavior. However, the crowd did as he had requested . . . they got naked! A riot was the result.[17]

Morrison also declared, "I'm god up there! I do what I want! I'm interested in anything about revolution, disorder, chaos, sex, and especially activity that has no meaning!" Nice guy, huh?[18]

The *late* Jimi Hendrix had an unusual act which caused crowd frenzy during his performances. He would place his guitar between his legs and stroke and strum violently until an "electronic climax" occurred among the thousands of fans.[19]

The Rolling Stones sing of a girl's menstrual period in the song "I Can't Get No Satisfaction." The line of the song which Jagger is always excited to perform says, ". . . who wants blood?" Mick said this was just life — why not write about it? "The kids with the clean songs are having a tough time having hits," he explained.[20]

The song "Rhapsody in the Rain," was banned from many radio stations in the late 1960's because of the explicit lyrics and the beat. It implied sexual intercourse in a car, making love to the rhythm of the windshield wipers. This song, as perverted as it is, is mild in comparison to the lyrics of today. Where are the people who were courageous enough then to try and do something about this audible smut? Where are they today?[21]

The Beatles recorded a "cute" little song which lasted one minute forty-two seconds and had only three lines. I mean, what can you say in three lines?? They said it! Repeated over and over are the words, "Why don't we do it in the road . . . no one will be watching . . . why don't we do it in the road?"[22]

Frank Zappa said in a *Los Angeles Times* interview, "A teenager can have his inhibitions lowered by music in the same manner as with pot, or heavier stuff." I thought about this for some time. Finally, an explanation of how this could happen was shared by Bob Larson in his book *Rock 'n Roll.* Mr. Larson, in conjunction with a physician, discovered that a person's blood sugar was directly affected by the driving bass beat in Rock music. The cerebrospinal fluid, which monitors the pituitary gland's secretion of adrenalin hormones, changes radically with the sound. This lowers the blood sugar which nourishes the brain. Consequently, moral inhibitions either drop to a dangerous low . . . or are completely wiped out. This explains why, as an ambulance driver I would work numerous auto accidents immediately following a rock concert. It also explains why "out of wedlock" pregnancies can be traced directly back to concert nights. This is not something to "fool around" with, to say the least. It's no joke!![23]

Rock music is the only education that many teens ever really experience. Not only has pornography been taught and caught, it has also been filmed. The Rolling Stones have made several films. The titles imply their content . . . "A Degree of Murder," "Tonight Let's Make Love in London," "Sympathy for the Devil," "Invocation of my Demon Brother," and "Cocksucker Blues." Of course, these should not be up for any kind of award.. . .unless Oscar is terribly ill. Nevertheless, some people obviously have access to this degrading imagery. Films could be the upcoming thing since the inception of MUSIC TELEVISION. MTV is the latest thing! It is visual radio on cable TV. The highest grossing Rock film was "Saturday Night Fever." It turned $74,000,000.

The term "ROCK 'N ROLL" came from a ghetto phrase which described sexual intercourse. It was coined by a New York disc jockey, Allen Freed. He began to refer to the "new music" as rock 'n roll in 1952. Since that time, it has definitely lived up to its original usage.

The exact scientific reason for why Rock music can arouse sexual instincts to a very dangerous level does not seem to be clear. However, many Rock stars claim to be able to turn on the "chicks" at will. It has been known for centuries that music can soothe or incite very deep-seated passions.

Many of today's songs leave nothing to the imagination as the songs of the '30's and '40's. Love does not mean romance as it once did. To present day performers it means *sex.* Meaningful relationships are seen as fruitless and filled with pain. For example, in the song "Two Out of Three Ain't Bad," the singer talks of his rejection from a lover's bed. He is assured that he is sexually attractive, but that *love* is out of the question. Real love involves commitment!

In other words, in today's music love is equated with lust. Rock stars sing of their own sexual philosophies. They are "hot blooded," and very much alert to the fact that "tonight's the night." They are one-night-standers! Only the act itself is important. Should one wonder why two out of three marriages in this country end in divorce? Some of the lyrics to the songs over the last few years should give marriage counselors a logical place to find some answers to this horrible dilemma. Try these titles: "I'm So Hot For Her," "I'd Really Like to See You Tonight," "Let's Make a Baby," "Lay Down, Sally," "Sharing the Night Together," "Afternoon Delight," "Nobody Does it Better," "Oh, What a Night," "Do Something Freaky," and "I'm in You."

Also, parents, there is a code language by which the more intimate details of human sexuality are explained. *THE god OF ROCK* is well aware that his messengers must carefully circumvent some lyrics in order not to bring Mom and Dad down too heavily on his parade. Terms like transmission, pumping gas, engine, motor or machine, hot oil, funky, groupie, get offs, and other euphemisms are used to convey explicit sexual experiences. Sex-oriented tunes are referred to as prophylactic or masturbatory Rock by industry insiders. Many of the more popular groups are turning to sado-masochism (the inflicting of pain for sexual stimulation and pleasure) for their latest thrill. The Rolling Stones in their album "Some Girls" sing songs such as "When the Whip Comes Down" and "Beast of Burden."

Most of the performers of Rock will admit that SEX is "where it's at." This is the selling force of their mainstream music. Actual physiological tests have even been conducted that indicate sexual excitement caused by sound. These tests, in some cases, have been the criterion for whether a song will be recorded or not. Women are portrayed as objects . . . men are depicted as exploiters . . . and music is declared to be synonymous with sex!

As shocking as this may seem, the fact of the matter is that most parents haven't the "foggiest" notion of what their children are listening to! Worse yet, parental ignorance goes as far as giving permission to an open display of this pornographic material in their homes. If this ignorance continues, *THE god OF ROCK* will most certainly empower his messengers to steal the values of our youth. The result?? You tell me!

Lest one were to think that the vehicle of Rock music does not carry the message of sexual promiscuity, let us share some of the songs that appear in the Book of Rock List of all-time greatest songs about masturbation: "The Beat," "Captain Jack," "Cool Jerk," "Dancing with Myself," "Fiddle About," "Jamaica Jerk-Off," "Pump It Up," "Rocks Off," "Slippery Fingers," and the infamous "Whip It."

Parents, I don't apologize . . . I am under mandate to inform!

Rock and rebellion are two peas in the same pod. The seedbed of the '50's laid the groundwork for the stormy '60's through the means of music. The country was ripe for revolution, and then came The Beatles singing "Revolution #9."

Was the British band invasion planned? Was it orchestrated? Did the Marxist brand of Communism know what would work against us? Did the godless of the globe target America for annihilation? Digest the following facts, and judge for yourself!

Mick Jagger declares, "If Jesus had been indicted in a modern court, he would have been examined by doctors, found to be obsessed by a delusion, declared incompetent and incapable of pleading his case, and sent to an asylum." Jagger is a graduate of The Fabian Socialist's London School of Economics. The school is very anti-Christ and very pro-Communist.[24]

John Lennon used a Marxist approach to dethrone God in the song, "Imagine." The order of the lyrics destroys all concepts of heaven and hell . . . takes down all forms of religion . . .

wipes out national sovereignty . . . and finally, eliminates any thoughts of ownership, such as private property, etc.[25]

Derk Taylor, former press secretary for The Beatles declared, "Here are four Liverpool lads who are rude, profane, vulgar, yet they have taken over the world. It's as if they have founded a new religion. They are completely anti-Christ. So much so, they shock me! This is not easy to do." And some thought they were clean-cut boys.[26]

John Lennon wrote in his *A Spaniard in the Works,* "Jesus is a garlic-eating, stinking, little yellow, greasy fascist bastard, Catholic Spaniard."[27]

Lennon also said, "Christianity will go! It will shrink and vanish! I needn't argue about that. I'm right, and will be proven so. We are more popular than Jesus right now!" He said this in August of 1966. He's dead . . . Jesus lives![28]

The *Denver Post* recorded the cry of The Beatles' fan club as being, "JOHN! NOT JESUS! JOHN! NOT JESUS!"[29]

George Harrison contended, "There is much more validity to Hinduism than anything in Christianity!" *The Chicago Tribune* reported The Beatles as having an extremely powerful influence on America's youth to turn from Christianity to other religions, and then from religion to Marxism and Communism.[30]

Think back with me if you will. The late '60's and early '70's were marked by violence and protest marches. Young people around the world were bordering on anarchy. What kept the anger at the boiling point? What was the driving force that was causing this eruption which so many times turned into tragedy? YOU GUESSED IT ... ROCK MUSIC! In 1970 Ohio National Guardsmen shot and killed four students at Kent State University during a protest riot. Where did that violent seed originate? How was it planted in the minds of these young people? How did the country continue to be stirred toward revolution? YOU GOT IT! ROCK MUSIC!

Listen to the titles of some of the more popular songs of that era. "Abraham, Martin and John," "Bad Moon Rising," "A Change is Gonna Come," "Don't Call Me Nigger No More, Whitey," "Stop, What's That Sound," "Games People Play," "Give Peace a Chance," "I Ain't Marching No More," "People Get Ready," "Revolution," "Street Fighting Man," "This is My Country," "Viet Nam," "A Bomb in Wardous Street," "Machine Gun," "Oliver's Army," "Peace Train," "Universal Soldier," "Anarchy in the U.K.," "Bring the Boys Home," "The Call Up," "We Have Control," "I'm So Bored with the USA," "Imagine," "Volunteers," "Waiting for the World to End," "War," "White Riot," "The World is a Ghetto," "English Civil War," "Fox Hole," "Life During Wartime," "War Pigs," "Your Flag Decal Won't Get You into Heaven Anymore."

These are only a few of the overwhelming number of protest songs recorded in the '60's and early '70's. As has already been said, it is a wonder that we survived the onslaught at all. This is assuming that we HAVE SURVIVED! Rock music became the primary vehicle for rebellion and revolution which was fostered from the outside and continued throughout these terrible times.

According to Ezekiel 22:26, a portion of the blame for this must be placed upon the parents, pastors and others in leadership roles. However, now that we can see what a powerful weapon music can be, we certainly should not simply sit by at present and do nothing!

The song "Street Fighting Man" by The Rolling Stones has a line which says, "The time is right for violent revolution!" The song was written in the latter '60's. However, it was this song that opened a concert in Dallas, Texas, in 1981. Jagger is still pumping out the poison . . . kids are still soaking it up!

Pete Seger, a Marxist folksinger once said, "The guitar is more powerful than the bomb." He could be right![31]

Dr. David Noebel relates an interesting observation in his book *The Marxist Minstrels.* He says, "Rome burned while a fiddle was playing. But, the United States might well burn to a bass, drums and screaming guitars."[32]

Martin Perlich, a Vice President of Disc Records, says, "Rock music has radicalized the majority of the young and has estranged them from the traditional virtues which they no longer see as relevant. Such things as marriage, country, religion, and the rest of the established social standards."[33]

Destruction seems to be the ultimate goal of the message of the Rock scene. Violence, rebellion toward all forms of authority, and rage are the normal "dress of the day." If a concert does not end with some fierce display designed to tear down the establishment, it was not successful . . . that is to the fans. As long as the money is in hand, the promoters are satisfied! But the hard core Rock fan must see blood! This is the obvious reason for the blatant aggrevation of the more popular groups. In order to be successful as a concert draw, they must do something bizarre . . . and they do!

For example, The Who destroys all of their instruments and a good portion of the stage at the conclusion of each concert. Keith Emerson of Emerson Lake and Palmer burns his Hammond organ during a grand finale of his appearances. The Plasmatics explode a car . . . and on we could go! There is seemingly no restraints placed upon the destructive tendencies of the performers. Consequently, the fans pay for whatever their idol's depraved nature desires.

Some of the most violent stage acts include Alice Cooper, Iggy Pop and the Stooges, Jerry Lee Lewis, Kiss, the MC5, The Dead Boys, The Move, and several others. These groups know just how to walk that fine line between crowd frenzy and riot. They can take an audience to a peak and keep them there until they become an angry mob ready to do whatever the musicians demand. It is at this point that the performers feel they have accomplished their purpose. If this is not Satanic . . . what is it!

Listen to these interesting facts about the destructive power of Rock music.

Music Professor Frank Garlock states in his book entitled *Voice*, "Rock music promotes neurotic behavior, revolution, teen wars, sex orgies, and riots. Because of the construction of the music such as repetition, no melody, notes under pitch, unnatural accents, and breaking up of rhythms, it is little wonder kids scream, faint, and go into convulsions."[34]

In a 1970 article entitled *Music that Kills Plants,* T. Olga Curtis related an experiment that had been carried out by a Denver woman. "For two years now, Mrs. Dorothy Patallack of Denver has been killing off plants by making them listen to Rock music. If this is the case, what is it doing to human teenagers? Mrs. Petallack played Led Zeppelin and Vanilla Fudge records to beans, squash, corn, and morning glories for three weeks. The result was that after 10 days, all of the plants were leaning away from the speakers. At the end of the three weeks, all of the plants were dying. Mrs. Petallack reversed the process sometime later, and played calm music to her plants for the same amount of time. She recorded a marked change. The plants drew toward the speakers and flourished."[35]

With the plant experiment in mind, meditate on this for awhile! The *New York Times* recently reported that 87 percent of America's teens listen to Rock music.[36]

Composer Andre Previn stated, "The closer that rock songs are to the idiot level, the more airway play they get and the better they sell." He is right, you know![37]

Eastern mysticism is an integral part of Rock music and is deeply entrenched in the lives of some of those who perform it. Musicians who have been directly influenced by the Maharishi Mahesh Yogi and Transcendental Meditation are The Beach Boys, The Rolling Stones, The Beatles, Skip Spence of Moby Grape, Earth Wind and Fire, and Jimi Hendrix, to name a few.

Several Eastern cults have their idolatrous roots in Pete Townshend of The Who, Seals and Crofts, Carlos Santana, The Moody Blues, Donovan, The Rascals, and George Harrison of the former Beatles. These are some of many. Lest parents have to learn to deal with alien thought forms and de-program their children, there should be a thorough investigation of the albums in the house!!

We are reminded of the terrible tragedy of Jonestown. Music played a vital part in the seduction of many young minds. Consequently, the bodies followed Jim Jones in a horrible suicidal death. This is said to be the ultimate expression of love and devotion. The Blue Oyster Cult sings a song entitled "The Reaper" which is a suicide pact between lovers. You see, the vehicle of Rock music is being used to siphon our youth and condition them to accept things that are diametrically and diabolically opposed to Biblical truth.

Some of the Eastern gurus who have had their teachings personified in wax include Gurdjieff, Krishna, Meher Baba, Subud, Sri Chinmoy, and others of a similar nature. It would take a scholar in world religions to be able to pinpoint the various advocations of alien gods in the lyrics and messages of Rock music. It seems that if Rock stars do not have a god of some kind . . . they simply find some religion or philosophy to embrace. This inevitably comes out in their music.

The most aggressive god is, of course, THE god OF ROCK himself. Satan's overwhelming desire is to be worshipped. He has certainly come out in the open through the performance of Rock. How many parents would allow a Satanic Bible by their young person's bedside? How many would allow a school teacher who was a self-professing and practicing witch to teach their children in a classroom? How many would turn a head if their kids were mixing potions and calling up demons? Most parents would certainly not allow this activity to gain ground in the lives of their most precious possessions . . . their children — that is, if they knew it!! Well, parents . . . WAKE UP!!! Listen to the startling facts.

The worship of the occult is exploding onto today's scene. How? Rock music is a primary vehicle. There are Rock bands who blatantly advocate the worship of Satan and magic. Fleetwood Mac publishes their music under a company named The Welsh Witch Publishing Company. Lead singer, Stevie Nicks, dedicates many of their concerts to all of the witches of the world. They sing of demons . . . and are said to be themselves the core of a coven. The Eagles band was formed on the occultic teachings of Carlos Castaneda. They sing of spirits, witches, the devil, possession, and other diabolical material. The Jefferson Starship's song "Light the Sky on Fire" is dedicated to Satan. Deep Purple held seances under the leadership of Richie Blackmore (now with Rainbow), a leading proponent of the occult. Jimmy Page, of Led Zeppelin, owns a large occult bookstore in London and is a follower of Aleister Crowley, an infamous British spiritualist. Daryl Hall of Hall and Oats is also a follower of the teachings and practices of Aleister Crowley. Todd Rundgren admits to astro travel in the arms of the "great one." The group Nazareth pictures demon manifestations on their album "Hair of the Dog." Ozzy Osborne claims to have had personal encounters with demons, and, of course, his former group, Black Sabbath, sings about the same type of experiences. Black Sabbath offers an invitation to follow Satan at the conclusion of some concerts. Uriah Heep recorded an album called "Demons and Wizards" which features a variety of occultish songs. Their latest album "Abominog" pictures an artist's conception of Satan on the cover. The Rolling Stones seem to be the embodiment of the darker messages of THE god OF ROCK. Their album "Goat's Head Soup" was recorded at a Haitian voodoo ritual. They have other songs and albums which obviously state their affiliation with their god, such as "Dancing with Mr. D." and "Sympathy for the Devil." The Stones' songs have been used in the Satanist's churches all across this nation.

"SATANIST'S CHURCHES," you say!! Oh yes . . . didn't you know? They are in every major city in this country. The question is, dear reader, who are you going to serve? Who is really your Lord? If you worship these performers . . . they are your gods. If you are committed to Rock 'n Roll . . . you will do what your gods espouse! You see, all occultish phenomenon comes from Satan who is the archenemy of the only true God. If you follow his messengers, your ultimate worship is to him (Satan).

Should the Christian continue to support the crusade of the greatest enemy of Jesus Christ? I think not! You may not be consciously affected, but the mind is like a computer. It will catalog the information, and the adversary will use it against you in the future. Please beware!

Another interesting study concerning the subject of Rock music involves *album cover art.* It was one of the most enlightening projects that was necessary for the production of this material. I could not believe my eyes! There are visual depictions of ALL FIVE of the major themes of Rock so clearly portrayed that one could know at a glance what the message is hidden in the grooves on the inside. Although there would be absolutely no possibility for this subject to be covered in detail, let us share some of what the research turned up. For example ...

The original cover of The Rolling Stones album "Beggar's Banquet" pictures a filthy restroom with vulgar graffitti on the walls. Among the dirty captions one sees written immediately above a gross-looking toilet, "God Rolls His Own." Very edifying, huh?

The cover of the John Lennon, Yoko One album "Two Virgins" pictures John and Yoko posed in the nude. There is a full frontal on the front of the cover and a full posterior on the back of the cover. Who wants to see that?

The cover of the 1971 Grank Funk Railroad album "Mom's Apple Pie" features an innocent looking matron holding out a steaming pie with a single slice removed. Rather than an apple or cherry filing, what the slice revealed was a vagina. Real creativity ... but clearly lascivious.

The album by the group Boxer entitled "Below the Belt" features a boxing glove slamming into a nude, spread-eagle female squarely in the crotch. This album was supposedly banned! It is still around!

The Jimi Hendrix album "Electric Ladyland" pictures Hendrix surrounded by at least a dozen voluptuous, but extremely nude women. Most of the women are white, as this seemed to be the strange sexual attraction attributed to Jimi.

The album "Head Games" by Foreigner, recorded in 1979, features a young woman sitting on a wall urinal in a men's restroom. Of course, this picture seeks to inspire bisexuality. So, what's new?

The Rolling Stones album "Sticky Fingers" pictures a close-up of a young man's crotch. He is wearing blue jeans with a zipper. The zipper really works! In fact, unzipping the zipper is how one gets into the album. Please imagine a young teenage daughter opening the cover to this recording. The title "Sticky Fingers" is more than suggestive!

The album "Come On and Get It" by Whitesnake portrays an innocent-looking apple that glistens with a transparent skin. Inside the apply is a snake that is coiled and ready to strike. An amusing take off on Eve, I'm sure!

The cover of Iron Maiden's album "Killers" pictures the skeleton of a Rock musician roaming the streets with a hatchet dripping with blood.

Another cover for Iron Maiden's album "The Number of the Beast" pictures this same skeleton watching over hell itself. The artist was very graphic about what it must be like. Demons and women were serving as the guards of the madhouse of the universe.

The album entitled "Virgin Fugs" by the Fugs pictures a photograph from underneath a young woman jumping over an object. It is very revealing, to say the least!

The album "If You Want Blood, You've Got it" by AC⚡DC pictures a member of the group with a guitar neck rammed through his stomach and blood splattered all over the stage. Please refrain from looking at this one until after meals!

The album "Aerosmith Live" features the winged globe used in the worship of the Egyptian sun god Ra.

The cover of the Black Sabbath album "The Mob Rules" pictures a grotesque torture rack wired like an electric chair and a gas chamber. It has a cross hanging from one side, depicting the crucifixion, and a shroud in the center, symbolic of Christ. Blood is splattered all over the rack, the floor, and the wall behind. Witches are portrayed as being the ones in charge of the torture. This one will get ya!!!

All of the albums of The Blue Oyster Cult picture their logo ... a Satanic cross.

On the cover of the David Bowie album "Chameleon" Bowie is pictured as half man and half woman. Bowie is a leader in the homosexual movement in the world of Rock.

The album entitled "Dream Police" by Cheap Trick pictures the group dressed in white and all surroundings in white as if they were in a dream. One of the members of the group is holding a chain saw with which he has just dismembered a female figure hanging from the ceiling. Really neat, guys!

The album "Slowhand" by Eric Clapton pictures a hand on the neck of a guitar featuring the middle finger salute. Some of the songs include "Cocaine," and "Finger Pie." Nothing left to the imagination, huh??

Alice Cooper's album "Muscle of Love" (clear enough?) comes wrapped in brown paper as if it were pornographic material coming in the mail. Well ... it is!

The album by Daryl Hall and John Oats entitled the same name has one guy dressed like a woman and the other like a man.

Heart's album "Little Queen" features a gypsy setting, complete with fortune teller, witch and crystal ball.

The album cover of Elton John's "Goodbye Yellow Brick Road" is a portrayal of John stepping from the real world into a gay world. This is reported to be an advocation for homosexuals to come out of the closet.

The album "Freeze Frame" by the J. Geils Band pictures an abstract person on the couch of a psychiatrist who is seen as a potato head. The person is looking in three different directions for answers ... to money, to an escape cop-out (drugs or alcohol), and to the occult. This one is symbolically weird!

On the cover of Genesis' album "A Trick of the Tail" there are various depictions of Alice in Wonderland with demonic characterizations.

Uriah Heep's newest "Abominog" pictures what the artist thinks the devil looks like. This one is really weird!

The Grand Funk Railroad album entitled "Survivor" has the boys eating raw meat on the cover. I guess if you are hungry, you'll do anything.

The Grateful Dead use a skeleton as their logo on all of their covers.

On the cover of Judas Priest's album "Sin After Sin" there is a temple of an alien deity with a skull at the top of the entrance, and a prostitute lying very suggestively on the floor, so as to lure one inside. This one is scary!

On the cover of the Kansas album "Audio Visions" two women are pictured with their tongues grossly extended. The real horror is that the women are personifications of stereo earphones. This is sexually seductive and demonic at the same time.

All Kiss albums feature the sado-masochistic garb of these demented child stealers.

The group Lucifer's Friend has the cover of its album "Mean Machine" literally splashed with Satanic symbols. Their name declares their allegiances.

The album "Bat Out of Hell" by Meat Loaf depicts a motorcycle emerging from hell with the rider being turned loose to inflict torment on the earth. This cover is demonic from corner to corner.

The group Molly Hatchet put out an album entitled "Take No Prisoners." Pictured on the cover is the group riding a red serpent dragon. Now what could this mean? Read the *Revelation* and find out!

The album cover for Nazareth's "Hair of the Dog" could not have been done by anyone without occult knowledge. It is very demonic!

The Plasmatic's album "Beyond Valley" pictures Wendy O. Williams in the buff from the waist up in several different pictures. Nudity is the name of the game on this cover.

There is so much that could be deciphered in the phenomenon of album art. For example, there is enough symbolism involving eastern religions that one could compile a fairly comprehensive work on that subject alone. Now here is the fly in the ointment. Anyone can purchase this material!! All a child must do is be able to reach the records on the racks and the counter at the check-out stand. *THE god OF ROCK* is definitely out to steal our children.

QUOTES

As has already been stated, the attitude of the messengers of *THE god OF ROCK* is more caught than taught! The lifestyle of the musicians themselves seems to be the determining factor of just how effectual their communication really is. They ingeniously address the most prominent issues of our time with calculated degeneration. The so-called "stars" seek to illuminate areas of life to which only their *god* would have the audacity to even refer.

According to II Corinthians 11:14 the adversary has the capacity to manifest himself as "light." Of course, he projects FALSE light ... but only the spiritually mature would recognize what is really happening! Some of the direct quotes by the trendsetters for the "now kids" should be sufficient to reveal how the new computers (young minds) are being programmed. The following represent only a tip on the proverbial iceburg! Some of the language is not printable in a book of this nature, so we have "Bleeped it out."

"Seriously, my only ambition in the world is to go to Egypt, stand on the top of the central pyramid, and p--- all over it." This was said by Ozzy Osborne[38]

"We are not anti-Christ ... just anti-pope and anti-Christian. Jesus is dead." Ringo Starr[39]

"I can see the devil and I'm Lucifer. Hey, it's a Satanic world!" Geezer Butler, bassist for Black Sabbath.[40]

"No one can really understand our lyrics unless they are out of their brain on something, and can build pictures in their minds." Alan White of Yes.[41]

"I formed this group as a personal protest against Anita Bryant and to make gays more acceptable in our society." Jacques Morali of The Village People.[42]

"We want to shock and be totally outrageous. On stage I'm a devil." Freddy Mercury of Queen.[43]

"I may go mad several times a year." Freddy Mercury of Queen.[44]

"I've had my allotment of liquor and drugs ... and probably 20 other people just like me." Grace Slick of the Jefferson Airplane/Starship.[45]

"I do all of my songs in one take, two at the most ... after that I'm tired of them! A song's just like a woman." Jerry Lee Lewis[46]

"We probably seem to be anti-religious. It's

simple! None of us believe in God!" Paul McCartney of the Beatles.[47]

"If God is hot stuff, why is He afraid to have other gods before Him?" Gene Simmons of KISS.[48]

"We did a gig at the Marquee once, the loudest we've ever done. I got home and put on "Blow by Blow" by Jeff Beck, and I couldn't hear the guitar playing at all. The whole top end of my ears were gone!" Eddie Clarke of Motorhead.[49]

"Since I've supposedly kicked the heroin habit, I've been asked to give a lecture to nearly 800 judges. What would I say to a bunch of f------ judges?? This would be the chance I've been waiting for ... I would say, 'F--- YOU!!' " Keith Richards of The Rolling Stones.[50]

"When I perform, I find myself evil! I believe in the devil as much as I do God. You can use either to get things done!" Peter Criss of KISS.[51]

"The songs come 'en masse' as if we are only a willing open medium." Keith Richards of The Rolling Stones.[52]

"Rebellion is the basis for our group. Some of the kids who listen to us are really deranged, but they look up to us as heroes because their parents hate us so much!" Alice Cooper.[53]

"Basically, I've always felt that I was a woman in a man's brain. I have seemed to be a man trapped inside a woman's body. I always had the initiative of a man, but was treated like some idiotic creature ... some little f------ beauty." Debborah Harry of Blondie.[54]

"My next song will be about death, hell and destruction in the third world." Sheena Easton[55]

"I perform best with a shot of smack (heroin) in each arm as opposed to eating too much!" Linda Ronstadt[56]

"I have boundless agony! I have boundless anguish! I have enough anguish, anxiety and despair to fuel at least another 10 to 15 years of career like this!" Leonard Cohen[57]

"At school I was supposed to be a clean cut kid, and have good grades. But ... all I wanted to do was get with the group that smoked joints in the back room!" Pat Benatar[58]

"Pop music is a popular method of conditioning the way people think!" Graham Nash of Crosby, Stills and Nash.[59]

"We're moving into the minds and so are most of the newer groups." Mick Jagger of The Rolling Stones.[60]

"In the Bible they blew horns and the walls of the city crumbled! Well, punk rock is like that!" Joe Strummer of the Clash.[61]

"In 1969 Kim Fowley called me up one day and asked very simply, 'Are you prepared to wear black leather, have sex with hundreds of teenage girls and get rich?' I said YES!" Warren Zevon[62]

"There isn't much difference between playing Rock 'n Roll and teaching in a school. You are both entertaining delinquents!" Sting of the Police.[63]

"I figured the only thing to do was to swipe their kids. By saying that, I'm not talking about kidnapping; I'm just talking about changing their value systems, which removes them from their parents' world very effectively." David Crosby of Crosby, Stills, and Nash.[64]

"I used to read my mother's porno magazines when I was nine, and I guess they interested me more than the Hardy Boys." Prince.[65]

"Apollo taught me to fly. Oh, how he taught me to live! Some day I'll be so complete I won't even be human. I'll be a god. Apollo is the major deity of the sun, moon and stars." John Denver[66]

"We've got all of the freaks on our side!!" Doug Saham of the Sir Douglas Quintet.[67]

"I'm not the ultimate study, but I'm pretty good at it. I've had plenty of practice. I mean, I'll have anybody's old lady ... I'm not proud!" Lemmy of Motorhead.[68]

"Sex is still the main motivation of my music! I find it a very positive thing ... in all of its forms!!" Adam Ant.[69]

"I just love drinking and getting stoned. I'll drink or do anything. I'm really not as mad as everyone makes me out ... I'm worse!" Ozzy Osbourne of the Blizzard of Oz.[70]

"Living on the brink of disaster at all times is what Rock 'n Roll is all about!" Kevin Cronin of REO Speedwagon.[71]

"A person who has rock music in their life has in their subconscious an influence that will cancel out all the power of the Word of God and the power it can have in your life. I don't doubt that if we don't take a stand against rock music that in twenty years there will not remain a Christian with a testimony for the Lord Jesus Christ!" Frank Garlock, author of *The Big Beat.*[72]

When Rock musicians are interviewed, they usually hold nothing back. I would not attempt to print some of the quotes uncovered in research. The purpose for any quotes at all is to allow the reader to know something of what the messengers of *THE god OF ROCK* are saying in their private lives. They address such things as abortion, economics, evolution, homosexuality, national defense, sex education, pornography, politics, and religion. Please believe me ... from what I've read, their knowledge is extremely limited. However, Rock music has become the major classroom in England and America. Young people wake up to its espousals and go to bed to its advocations. Very few teens do not immediately reach for the radio knob when they get into a car. The prince of the power of the air never sleeps. He is bent on destroying God's people, and the church is doing very little about it!

TRACKS

There is a code language being expressed through the vehicle of Rock that the uninitiated do not "pick up." The hypesters are busy sharing their destructive message, and only a few really understand what is being said. However, please remember that the subconscious mind, which is the seat of the soul, is still affected. Just as the anointing of the Holy Spirit can affect the soul with an edifying message, Satan can convey a counterfeit function which can stifle and create an unhealthy spiritual atmosphere. There is great power behind the creative impulses of musical performers. This has Biblical basis as seen in the case of King David. Music can facilitate the presence of the Holy Spirit, or conjure up demons through rhythmic repetition and idolatrous devotion. Hence, it is not absolutely necessary for one to understand what is being said to be damaged by it!

For example, here are only a *few* of the TRACKS that are conveying messages that say something other than what the average listener may think.

Simon and Garfunkle's song "Bridge Over Troubled Water" speaks of a "silver girl." This is teenage slang for a hypodermic needle. This song is about a heroin addict and his pusher, and I have actually heard it sung in church portraying Christ as "the bridge." Remember, that was certainly not the intent of the writer. The power lies in their intent, not ours!

The Bee Gees' song "The Edge of the Universe" speaks of "Shanendorah," which in the spirit world means out of the body to the edge of the universe. The Bee Gees have admitted that their music was blessed by Satan. One confesses to a hobby of pornographic drawing, while the others lay claim to psychic powers.

Tod Rundgren and Utopia recorded an album entitled "Ra." The lyrics had their base in Japanese and Egyptian mysticism. Few who listen would be consciously aware that they were receiving false religious data.

Gary Wright and his popular song "Dream Weaver" tells us how to float among the astral planes. This is an out-of-the-body experience. "What is the harm in that?" you ask. It is strongly opposed to Biblical truth! Isn't that enough?

Stevie Wonder's song "Jesus, Children of America" cuts down Christianity and glorifies Transcendental Meditation as the way to find peace of mind.

The song "Serpentine Fire" by Earth, Wind and Fire is based on the spinal life energy system found in the Shah Kriza Yogi Meditation Cult. This group joins hands before each concert in order to enter into the proper transcendental state.

The song 'Rhiannon" by Fleetwood Mac is about a witch in Wales.

Heart's song "Devil's Delight" speaks of a dirty daughter demon delight that screams and dances through the night.

John Denver's song "Rocky Mountain High" refers to a born-again experience. This sounds great on the surface! However, Denver said in an interview concerning the meaning of the lyrics that he sees himself as a sort of messiah and is using his music to being in a new secular religion. The leaders of this new religion claim to control the universe and claim to be gods.

The Village People's song "YMCA" says that gays should go to the the YMCA because "...it is a good place to have fun with all the boys." I thought YMCA stood for Young Men's Christian Association! Please deliver me!

Queen's song "Bohemian Rhapsody" says, "...Beelezebub has a demon set aside for me." This is probably the only date you could get, Freddy!

The Beatles song 'I am a Walrus" uses backward masking to advocate the use of pot. Their songs "Hey, Jude," "Fixing a Hole," and "Lucy in the Sky with Diamonds" are, according to Time Magazine, DRUG DRENCHED.

The album "Agents of Fortune" by The Blue Oyster Cult contains songs which relate to various subjects involving witchcraft ... such as "...he who comes against the power faces death." The power, of course, is Satan!

Led Zeppelin's song "Trampled Under Foot" uses the sexual code language to refer to intercourse. It speaks of a girl's transmission as having hot oil flowing, and the guy who would like to pump some gas! In other words ... let's "get it on." She's hot for him ... and he's ready for her!

Billy Joel's song "Only the Good Die Young" refers to young Catholic girls who remain virgins too long.

The Rolling Stones song "Am I Rough Enough" is talking about sado-masochism. Jagger sings of pain and pleasure.

Neil Diamond's very popular "Crackling Rose" is talking about a bottle of rose wine as being his woman.

The Rolling Stones' song "Dancin' with Mr. D." speaks of a graveyard romp with Satan himself as the partner. Personally, I would hope to do better than that!

The Jackson Browne song "Rock Me on the Water" declares reincarnation is certain. There is no doubt about it! It is a belief.

Stevie Wonder's award-winning "Songs in the Key of Life" was released in conjunction with his astrological advisors' approval and his personal sign Taurus. You see, there are other ways to dedicate music to Satan than just doing so in an obvious manner.

The Eagles' song "Witchy Woman" sings of a restless spirit who flies through the night with sparks shooting from her fingers.

Again, The Eagles sing of searching for the daughter of the devil in their million seller "One of these Nights."

George Harrison's song "My Sweet Lord" sings of Lord Krishna. Many people thought that Harrison became a Christian when this song came out. Far from it!

Harrison's song "Give Me Love" also refers to Hindu life cycles.

John Lennon's hit song "Instant Karma" has reference to the Hindu doctrine of cyclical retribution. It speaks of an attempt to avoid the process, and be at one instantly! He went somewhere instantly!! Guess where!!

The Beatles' song "Magic Carpet Ride" refers to a trip on LSD.

The Rolling Stone song "Sister Morphine" is a lyrical advocation to "get high" on the highest of all highs!!

The enormous hit by ZZ Top entitled "La Grange" is about a whorehouse. In fact, it is the whorehouse that is now being glorified in the movie, "The Best Little Whorehouse in Texas."

Bob Dylan's song "Rainy Day Woman" speaks of sitting at home smoking a joint and getting high with a woman who is shaped like a cigarette.

The tracks are endless. The meanings are overt, covert, subtle, obvious, clear, hidden, blatant, screened, simple, coded, blunt or latent ... BUT EVER PRESENT.

These LYRICS, FACTS, QUOTES AND TRACKS represent only a drop in the ocean. Rock music is probably the most dangerous vehicle of destruction ever devised and propagated upon the human race. It shoots straight for the center of control ... THE MIND. The manipulators of this calculated attempt to chisel away at the foundation are gaining momentum! America is heading downhill very rapidly. We are faltering morally because we have deserted the *Bible* which would give us the only sound *base* to exist as a free society. Truly, friends, America is fast creating a spiritual and sociological nightmare. Because of this, a new dark age could be just around the corner.

The Bible teaches that we should NOT GIVE HEED TO SEDUCING SPIRITS! (II Tim. 4:1)

CHAPTER SEVEN

ONE FINAL WORD!
(DO YA STILL THINK IT'S OKAY?)

YOUNG PEOPLE, WOULD YOU LIKE TO BE FREE FROM THE AWESOME POWER OF AND ADDICTION TO ROCK MUSIC?? You may have already made up your mind that you would like to stop listening to anything that does not glorify God. If so, I have good news! You can! However, maybe you are not thoroughly convinced that it is wrong to listen, or think that you can listen and not be affected. Following are several questions to ask yourself. It could be that you are on the borderline and you just need some food for thought.

Ask yourself, "Is the message that I am hearing from my favorite group or song full of truth? Is it godly?" The apostle Paul clearly states that we must place our minds upon things that are true. This is expressed in Philippians 4:8. The word *truth* in this verse means REAL. If what you are hearing is not *REAL*, take your mind off of it. There is so much make believe being put out by the pseudo-glitter of the Hollywood hype that it is hard for us to tell what is image and what is not. If the music to which you listen expresses things that are not actual or true in character, please be assured that the enemy is out to capture your mind. Gals, get out of that storybook concept of romance. Guys, wake up to the fact that the American dream is a hoax and that you cannot know anything that *is REAL* if your mind is upon that which is fake or false. Kids, start with a TRUE premise. The base for proper thinking is only found in the Word of God.

Ask yourself, "Is my music pure? Is it worthy? Does it promote praise? Is it admirable and respectful?" If it is not, as a Christian, you are under mandate to turn away. I know this is a hard statement to accept. Especially if you are heavily into Rock. However, anything that is not righteous and does not produce right conduct is against scriptural principles. Now, I am well aware that many will say, "So, what is the real problem? I mean, I got problems a lot worse than this!" Have you considered that Rock could be the root to all of your problems? Oh yes! It can greatly affect the mind, which causes abnormal behavioral patterns to develop that even *you* do not know from where they come.

Continue asking yourself, "When I listen to my music, does it cause me to want to avoid or embrace sexual immorality. Paul again states in II Timothy 2:22 that we are to flee youthful lusts. As you know by now, you are at your peak in sexual alertness. The desire of our youth is extremely powerful, and the enemy knows this. And -- he doesn't play fair. In fact, he cheats! This is the area where he hits us in full force. If the music you are hearing on a daily basis is stimulating lust, turn it off. Those basic drives are more than you can handle! Something will give and usually it's you that gets hurt.

Ask yourself, "Is my music causing division in the lives of those I love and those who love me?" In other words, kids, you live in one of the most affluent societies in history. The sweat that your parents pour out to provide and make life "easy" is often overlooked or seldom acknowledged. Why is it so hard for young people to give frequent expression of thankfulness? Why is it so hard to just say, "All right, Mom and Dad, I'll slow down on the music because I know it is a sore spot with you!"? After all, did Jimi Hendrix change your diaper? Did Jimmy Page feed you your bottle? Did Deep Purple buy your food? Did KISS put the roof over your head? Did Alice Cooper walk you through your childhood diseases? Of course not!! Mom and Dad did those things. Hey! If they ask you not to listen to that kind of music, that's enough. They don't have to understand all about it to tell you that. Just listen and obey. The scripture says that if you will, your life will be long on the earth. If your music is dividing your home or causing problems with your parents, STOP LISTENING TO IT. Who means the most to you? Your music or your parents? If you say music, you *DO* have a problem!

Continue asking, "Do I enjoy the evil and the sensuality that my music stimulates?" If you do, this could be the manifestation of more severe problems that Rock music is only bringing to the surface. Maybe there is excitement at the thought of torture or sadism. Maybe you have frequent thoughts of abnormal sexual activities. Listen, if music excites these types of feelings, DO NOT LISTEN ANYMORE! CUT IT OFF! You are headed for some serious trouble if you do not.

Further, ask, "Can I walk in the Spirit of God when I listen to my favorite group?" The scripture clearly teaches that if you have been *born in* Christ, you are to also *walk in* Him. If your music hinders this walk (lifestyle), then it is not good for you. If you subconsciously adopt the philosophy or lifestyle of some of the popular Rock stars, this is an affront to the Lord Jesus. In fact, if some Rock star is your lord, then Jesus is *not*. He has made it clear that He will not play second to anyone. You are either in submission to Him or to the star of your choosing. As Bob Dylan sings, "You gotta serve somebody."

Does your music cause you to go places you know are displeasing to God? Do you go to concerts? Do you place His temple in the atmosphere of what goes on at a concert just to hear and see your Rock idol? If so, this is against the exhortation and direct commands of the Bible. Oh, yeah! II Cor. 3:17 states that if the Spirit of God is not there, one does not honor God by being there himself. The motivation of the heart is known by God. And many wonder why their Christian lives are not up to the level they believe they ought to be. Little wonder, if you follow THE god OF ROCK.

Oh, there are many questions that you might ask in order to help you make up your mind if you should be listening to Rock. For instance: Does not the scripture teach that you are to flee the very appearance of evil? Are we not to think of other people and how they look at us? Should our testimony not be important?

Young people, you *DO NOT* have to follow the crowd. My pastor, Dr. Richard Kirgan, said recently, "If the crowd is doing it, according to Matthew 7:13, it is wrong, and will ultimately destroy you!" You ask, "What does Matthew 7:13 say?" Look it up. But remember ... if the crowd is doing it, it will lead to destruction.

There is no doubt that Rock music is destructive. If you are involved, it is just a matter of time before you, too, will feel its devastating power. Maybe you already have, and you want out! Great! There is a way.

The apostle Paul answers the problems, solves the dilemmas, cures the arguments and thoroughly addresses the issue in Philippians 4:8. I close this book with the admonition to read and heed this verse.

"Finally, brethren, whatsoever things are true, whatsoever things are honest, whatsoever things are just, whatsoever things are pure, whatsoever things are of good report; if there be any virtue, if there be any praise, THINK ON THESE THINGS."

A DEFINITION OF TERMS

Punk Rock - An outrageous type of musical debauchery. Punk is usually an outburst of garbled and unintelligible lyrics forcefully thrust to a drunken, surly, unruly mob of leather-bound mohawk-headed kids. This type of music calls for the most decadent forms of activity. Its real beginnings are American, but Great Britian brought it out of the "closet."

New Wave - New Wave is "high energy" disco music. High energy means very loud and full of heavy syncopated rhythms. This is the type of music used in gay bars and disco lounges.

Heavy Metal - Heavy metal is a term that refers to the electronic sound in Rock. It is a term that was defined by the English band Black Sabbath. Loud screaming guitar riffs with piercing feedback and hard repetitiously driving bass licks allows even the layman to recognize the bombastic form of hypnotism.

Riff - A guitar lick in the bridge or break of a song.

Formula - A proven sound. One that is commercial and marketable.

Driving - A hard drum or bass beat that tends to drive one to the ground.

Dissonance - The clashing of harmonies.

NOTES

THE PROOF OF THE PUDDING'

1. Jerry Rubin, Do It! (Simon and Schuster; New York) p. 19, 85, and 249.
2. Aristotle, Politics; p. 1339.
3. American Journal of Psychiatry, Vol. 99, Dr. Joyce Brothers.
4. "Seattle Daily Times," Aug. 22, 1964, p. 1.
5. Edward Hunter, *Brainwashing*; (Pyramid Books, N.Y.), p. 22.
6. "L.A. Herald Examiner," Aug. 8, 1965, p. 9.
7. *Henry David Thoreau*; (Walden Books, N.Y.), p. 147.
8. David Noebel, *The Marxist Minstrels*; (American Christian College Press, Tulsa, OK), p. 45.
9. Gene Lees, *Rock Violence and Spiro Agnew*; (High Fidelity, N.Y.), p. 108.
10. "Saturday Evening Post," March 25, 1967, p. 41.
11. "Cavalier," June 1968.
12. "Life," June 28, 1968.
13. "Life," June 16, 1967, p. 105.
14. "Crime in America," Oct. 23, 1969, p. 152.
15. "Time," Apr. 28, 1967, p. 53.
16. "Time," June 23, 1967, p. 43.
17. "Ft. Lauderdale News," Mar. 6, 1969.
18. "Newsweek," Nov. 6, 1967, p. 101.

19. Arnold Shaw, *The World of Soul*, (Cowles Book Co., N.Y.), p. 262.
20. "Time," July 1, 1966, p. 57.
21. "Time," July 8, 1966.
22. *The Beatles' Lyrics Illustrated*; (Del Pub. N.Y.)
23. "L.A. Times," Nov, 27, 1966.
24. William Foster, Toward Soviet America; (Elgin Enterprises, Inc. Cal.), p. 317.
25. Ib. 22.
26. "Saturday Evening Post," Aug. 8, 1964, p. 28.
27. John Lennon, *A Spaniard in the Works*; (Simon & Schuster, N.Y.), p. 14.
28. "N.Y. Times," Aug, 5. 1966, p. 20.
29. "Denver Post," Aug. 11, 1966, p. 65.
30. "N.Y. Times," Dec. 12, 1966, p. 57.
31. "Tulsa Daily World," Apr. 16, 1968, p. 8.
32. Ib. 8, p. 196.
33. "Cleveland Press," July 25, 1968, 1-M.
34. Frank Garlock, *Voice*, Vol. 40, 6, April 1967, p. 35.
35. "Denver Post," June 21, 1970, p. 8-M
36. "N.Y. Times," Aug. 28. 1970, p. 35.
37. "San Francisco Sunday Examiner," Sept. 25, 1966, p. 13.
38. *Rock Yearbook 1982*; (Saint Martins Press, N.Y.), p. 189.
39. "Playboy," Feb. 1965, p. 58.
40. "Rolling Stone," October 28, 1972, p. 41.
41. Ib. 28, p. 190.
42. "Newsweek;" Apr. 2, 1979.
43. "Circus," Apr. 1974, p. 41.
44. "Circus," Mar. 1977, p. 42.

45. Ib. 38.
46. Ib. 38.
47. Ib. 39.
48. "Circus," Sept. 1976, p. 42.
49. Ib. 38.
50. Ib. 38.
51. "Rolling Stone," Apr. 4, 1967, p. 49.
52. "Rolling Stone," May 5, 1977, p. 5.
53. "Circus," Feb. 1972, p. 61.
54. Ib. 38.
55. Ib. 38.
56. "Rolling Stone," Mar. 27, 1975.
57. Ib. 38.
58. Ib.
59. Ib.
60. Ib.
61. Ib.
62. Ib.
63. Ib.
64. "Rolling Stone," Apr. 1980.
65. Ib. 38.
66. "Newsweek," Dec. 20, 1976.
67. Ib. 38.
68. Ib.
69. Ib.
70. Ib.
71. Ib.
72. Frank Garlock, *The Big Beat*; (N.Y.)

BIBLIOGRAPHY

The Illustrated Encyclopedia of Rock, (Harmony Books; New York, New York 10016)
Who's Who in Rock, (Facts on File, Inc.; New York, New York 10016)
David A. Noebel, *The Marxist Minstrels;* (American Christian College Press, Tulsa, Okla. 74102.
The Beatles' Lyrics Illustrated; (Dell Publishing Co., New York, New York 10017).
The Rock Year Book 1982; (St. Martin's Press, New York, New York 10010).
The Year in Rock 1981-1982; (Delilah Books, New York, New York 10010).
Lowell Hart, *Satan's Music Exposed*; (Salem Kirban, Inc., Hunting Valley, Penn. 19006).
The Book of Rock Lists; (Dell Publishing Co.; New York, New York 10017).
Bob Larson, *Rock*; (Tyndale House Publishers, Inc., Wheaton, Illinois).
Magazines: Rolling Stone, Circus, Time, Newsweek, People, Hit Parade, Billboard, Cashbox.

ADDENDUM

"Rock Music is now, has been, and always will be the voice and language of he rebel", said a member of a currently faddish rock group to an early morning news anchor woman. I was personally astounded as she proceeded to glorify the group, but at the same time, I knew that what the young man said was most assuredly the truth. There is an unmistakable correlation between this form of music and the negative effect upon the attitude of the listeners.

Why is this the case, one might ask? The reason is really quite simple! Music is spiritual in origin and in design. Music literally touches a person's spirit, wherein lies the real source of creativity. In other words ... music is spiritual in it's effect. It calls one's attention to the root of worship. It was originally designed to breed and foster praise to God, and be the vehicle whereby the heavens would worship Him.

In light of what we are dealing with, this is an awesome thought. Why? Because so many rock stars have seen this universal principle and are calling attention to the arch enemy of God ... and not to the one true God. They are playing into the strategy of Satan and gaining worship for him from millions of fans who defend rock music even as it is destroying them. How subtle the Christian's adversary really is!

There are so many things that could be added to this addendum, but space will certainly not permit. Rock groups are emerging with an intensity that should cause even the nominal listener to be alarmed and dismayed. Style has been obliterated and formula music is now causing the promoter's cash registers to sound like burglar alarms. The music industry is "smoke-screening" the masses with a strategy insiders refer to as 'one record bands'. This simply means that a group comes out with one record and are never heard of again. The plan makes it very difficult for anyone to keep up with what is happening. However, as we have already stated, music is not the real problem—the root problem is lordship. In other words, who or what is in control of our lives is the question. We can readily determine this by who or what we defend. Whatever we defend is our god.

In the course of the next few pages we will attempt to make mention of some current groups and show anyone interested how to pay closer attention to their personal listening habits.

We have discovered that some of the main line bands mentioned in the preceeding chapters either partially own, or own outright, many of the newer groups. This behind the scenes propagation leads us to believe that the progression of the vehicle of rock music is here to stay until the Lord Jesus comes back for His own.

The newer bands, for the most part, are products of the United Kingdom. They have bombarded American fans with even more intensity than the British invasion of the sixties. This is largely due to America's video mania. Music television, and other videos are bizzare beyond description. What our young people are watching on television in their homes can be purchased in uncut versions at the local video stores. Parents . . . do not be fooled! It will not be long before the uncut versions will be shown during regular programming.

"I don't watch that stuff!", a parent might reply. You had better Mom and Dad ... You'd better! Music television is the most addicting form of mind control to ever hit this country. The money spent on the average videos is beyond what most of us could imagine, but the record companies know they will gain an impressive return on their money because of adult ignorance. These videos cause young people to be exposed to groups that even they could not stomach if it were not for their images being placed into their minds as they watch. Again we reiterate ... how subtle our enemy is!

There are two scriptures, among many, that we believe should not go unheeded. First, in 1 Samuel 15:23 the Bible clearly teaches that *rebellion* is as the sin of *witchcraft*. Please notice! Rebellion is the very heart and core of the rock music world, and God views rebellion in the same manner that he does *witchcraft*. In other words, if a person is caught up in an attitude of rebellion, God does not take it lightly. He looks upon that person as a follower of Satan and his craft. This is serious and extremely dangerous, especially for the Christian.

The second scripture that we should be very careful not to overlook is found in Deuteronomy 7:25-26. This passage teaches that a child of God is not to bring any objects of worship other than those relating to the one true God into their homes.

Now, let's get serious! Young people DO worship rock musicians. Bedroom walls are full of posters, etc. Tee-shirts manifest where allegiance really is. Concert trophies are too numerious to mention. For a truth, rock musicians have become gods to the vast majority of their fans. In fact, the word fan has the same root meaning as the word follower. This is interesting because Jesus used the word follower in relationship to our following *Him*. He did not teach that we could be a fan or a follower of other gods . . . only Him. This is the underlying problem. Rock musicians are used to trick their fans, addict their fans, and distract their fans from Jesus.

Kids, this scripture simply says this: if we bring idols into our homes, we will become accursed in the same manner as they. The believer should utterly abhor and detest anything that distracts him from the knowledge of God which comes from spending time with Him rather than time with the world and the Gods thereof.

Please remember that it will be impossible to do anything but abbreviate the following information. Our intention is not to write another volume, but to share current facts that we believe to be pertinent in helping you determine the spiritual dangers in the Rock arena. Notice the names of the groups, where they come from, and how they have made such an abrupt inroad into the minds of our youth.

ADDENDUM TO GLOSSARY

A B C

Formed 1980 in United Kingdom ... founder was a former editor to the magazine "Modern Drugs" ... gained American audience through MTV ... album "Lexicon of Love" is sensual and blatent.

BAUHAS

Formed 1978 in United Kingdom ... heavily influenced by Iggy Pop and David Bowie, two bizzare performers ... a cult of followers in the English punk area ... occultish stage act.

BOOMTOWN RATS

Formed 1975 in United Kingdom ... made charts with single dealing with pathological homicide.

BOW WOW WOW

Formed 1980 in United Kingdom ... cloned to be sex pistols of the 80's ... genius for controversy and rebellion ... mohawk haircuts and sordid sex appeal ... father band for Boy George ... gained American audience through MTV.

JOHN COUGAR

U.S. composer singer whose music and performances provide a tailor made vehicle to deliver sex and rebellion. Songs include "I Need a Lover", "Nothin' Matters and What if it Did", "American Fool," and "Hurt So Good."

CULTURE CLUB

Formed in United Kingdom 1981 . . . founder is the effeminate Boy George . . . female impersonation, bisexuality, and rebellion leaves no one doubtful as to what they believe . . . amazing success coming in the garments of Sodom . . . much could be said concerning the implications that surround the success of this group. One would hope that they are not the mirror of society in America that they claim to be. How could an ex window dresser bi-sexual dress and act like a woman and take our country by storm? Think about it!

DEF LEPPARD

Formed in United Kingdom 1978 . . . another heavy metal band with screaming guitars and lyrics . . . began British tee-shirt craze . . . very popular among Jr. High youth because of rebellion advocated in music . . . album "Pyromania" smash hit in American market fanning the flames of rebellious attitudes among teens.

DURAN DURAN

Formed in United Kingdom 1980 . . . project a bi-sexual image . . . hit the American charts by means of strong sex oriented videos . . . appeals to very young following.

GIRL SCHOOL

Formed in United Kingdom 1978... Display image of rebel with appearance and music... heavy metal performed by women... albums include "Demolition", "Screaming Blue Murder"... violence spread to youthful female rock star hopefuls.

SAMMY HAGAR

U.S. singer composer with a flair for writing sexually suggestive lyrics... flamboyant or outrageous stage performance... standing as a personification of the rebel attitude, Hagar marches on.

MICHAEL JACKSON

U.S. singer with currently enormous platform of success... mirrors the current youth mindset... faces the danger of high level success... proported to be the Messiah by the Jehovah Witnesses... (Let's use a short formula to examine this superstar whose influence touches people from 4 to 60?). What we determine must be seen in light of scripture.

First, examine the *Man*—Portrays a bi-sexual image in appearance, voice, and clothes. Prone to deep states of depression and crying. Has become the idol of millions of teens... an object of worship. Should a man be worshipped?

Next, Examine the *Music*—Just a look at "Thriller" reveals to the casual observer how far young people have strayed from the Truth. In the first place, the Bible does not teach that ghouls will be resurrected from the dead, etc.

Next, Examine the *Motive*—This is a difficult part of the formula to apply to this singer. One has to wonder if humanistic success is not the under-lying thrust. God's glory or man's glory is the question.

Last, Examine the *Method*—There is no doubt that the greatest promotion minds of this age are behind the Michael Jackson mania. The worlds methods are inextricably bound up in success.

Christian young people and parents must think this one through in the light that comes only from the Word of God. Otherwise, because of the subtlety of this star phenomena, deceit will cloud the mind. No matter what the disclaimers about "Thriller" state, it is full of lies.

Also, Christians have always considered the Jehovah's Witnesses a cult, simply because they deny the diety of Christ. Again, worship is due on-ly to God and to His Son, Jesus, who died for the redemption of man. You see, because of the clean cut image of the Jacksons, a very subtle thing has happened. Be careful! Michael Jackson actually has the youth of America walking backward!

Apply the formula under the leadership of the Holy Spirit and see for yourself if what you observe in Michael Jackson matches up with the Word of God. Here is a perfect test case for examining our knowledge of Christ, and our relationship to Him. Who is more important to you? To whom do you owe your salvation? Even though Jackson's followers are messianic in numbers . . . Jesus is the Messiah, not Michael. Think and pray long and hard about this. I know the above statements may receive ins-tant disapproval, but remember, whoever you de-fend is your god.

GRACE JONES

West Indian singer composer ... embodies the bi-sexual concept ... bizzare stage act protraying sado-masochistic fantasy ... a picture of decadent sen-suality ... made popular by means of videos.

LOVERBOY

Formed in Canada 1979 ... clearly a bi-sexual heavy metal insufficiency ... songs of sexuality and rebellion fill their limited repertoire.

MOTLEY CRUE

This group is a reincarnation of Kiss ... bizarre stage garb and performance ... rebellion in rare form ... album "Shout at the Devil" calls for all of the children of the beast to rise up and fight ... their billing reads, "Every Mother's Nightmare" and they truly are ... full of sexual explicits and violence.

RATT

Currently popular video group ... rats to eat, rats to bring out the animal in women ... rats!

SCORPIONS

German group formed in 1970 ... heavy metal vehi-cle with combat rock approach ... currently popular due to video craze and album "Love at First Sting" ... group projects the familar straight for-ward advocation to rebel against authority and do what you feel.

38 SPECIAL

Formed in U.S. 1979 ... straight ahead rock with southern boogie flair ... founded in the Lynyrd

Skynrd tradition of bar room brawling and southern pride ... rebellion is the underlying theme as this group gains momentum.

TUBES

Formed in U.S. 1972 . . . Bizzare stage performances with semi nude girls and guys, if one can tell the difference . . . leather and chains indicate the sado masochistic makeup of the group ... appeared in porno movie . . . blatent sexism and rebellion.

As has been previously stated, rock groups are emerging at a pace that defies the average Christian to maintain awareness. The cruelty of the entertainment scene, however, leaves numerous tragedies. Murder for fun ... teenage suicide ... and other forms of ultimate destruction are advocated by bands and songs.

There is a reason for this. You see, the god of Rock could care less who serves him, as long as somebody does. Young musicians and their fans are being seduced into the diciplines of darkness and seem to be following without any real regard for themselves or a life of true peace and power. This is truly sad.

Some of the more recent groups, such as 'Twisted Sister', sings songs which clearly indicate that the battle lines are obvious. They say they will fight a thousand preachers to teach the youth of the world rebellion. Remember, the scripture informs the person who desires to follow Jesus that rebellion is as the sin of *witchcraft*! You cannot grow in your relationship with the Lord and listen to an avalanche of cursing words ... stop pretending!

Lucifer's goal has always been to call attention and worship to him. The Bible states in Isaiah 14, and Ezekial 28 (the two accounts of the creation of Satan) that musical instruments and light were built into Him. In other words, his being includes music and the ability to express it.

If you are interested in a further pursuit of what is really behind the success of the entertainment industry, which is a recent phenomenon, the Bible is not silent. The accounts mentioned teach that tabrets (tamborines), pipes (melodics), and viols (strings) were placed to Lucifer. Also he was extremely beautiful due to the precious gems fashioned in him which emanate light. He saw his beauty, and desired to receive the worship that was due to God alone. When God saw this in his thinking, the first war took place in the heavenlies. Lucifer rebelled and led one third of the angels in heaven against the sovereign God. He was kicked out of heaven, and became Satan. He fell to earth and was confined to the atmosphere in which we now live. In fact, he was given dominion over the atmosphere by God Himself. He was the first rebel, and is still in the business of calling attention and worship to himself and away from God. This is what he desired all along and he is achieving this in this century as never before.

Have you ever wondered why musicians have become gods? Have you considered what is behind the hype, the glitter, the glamor? Think! Music was originally designed to bring praise to God, and Lucifer was the one in charge of coordinating that praise. He desired the worship, however, and rebelled. Please do not take this lightly. Do not think of Satan as "the force", or some kind of "it". He is personal, real, and bent on the destruction of man who is made in the image of God. Listen, if he can deceive you, and distract you from God's plan and design for your life, he can "get back at God" in whose image you are made.

Many Christian young people will not admit that something or someone is in control of their lives other than the Lord or themselves. There is, however, a simple way to find out if this is true. Whatever could have even the possibility of control, other than Christ, do without it for a week. If you think that music does not control you, stop listening for seven days! Go on a seven day "media fast". Abstain from listening! The first thing you will discover is how addicted you are, and do not know it. The second thing the fast will do for you is clean your mind from negative data which causes rebellious attitudes. It is definitely a challenge, and has changed the lives of countless numbers of people.

Priority Publications has a book entitled *Life in the Fast Lane* which gives the reasons for the fast, and how to do it. Write if you need help.

Again, if you are not in full agreement with the thesis of this book, apply the formula for gauging your listening habits yourself. Get your Bible, take what you know about the group in question and examine carefully . . .

The Man

The Music

The Motive

The Method

Look at the performers personally and what they

stand for. Do not settle for opinions, allow the Word of God to say what it says. Then, listen to the message in the vehicle of the music. What is the lyrical content? Is it opposed to scripture? Does it teach rebellion, illicit sex, false god concepts, etc? Then, what is the motive? Is it purely money? If so, what does the Bible teach about this motive? Does the motive of the performers appear to glorify God or Satan? And how about the method . . . is it the worlds way? If it is, should the Christian young person, or anyone else who adorns the name of Jesus, be closely associated with it? You see, one can be condemned by association. It is a simple formula, and will apply to any form of music.

Young people are very street wise in this generation. Please do not let the world's wisdom dim the things that God has in store for those who love and serve Him. It is difficult to even imagine how hard it will be to break away from the bondage of Satan. However, the power to do it will be given by God Himself to those who desire to know Him with all their heart. If you choose to stand firm for Christ in these trying times, you will experience only a glimpse of what it was like for Him to die alone for the sins of mankind. This stance, however, will cause you to develop a love relationship with Jesus that supercedes anything to be found in all of the world.